The Treaty of Nice

One
day loan

Please return on or before the last date
stamped below.
Charges are made for late return.

The Treaty of Nice and Beyond

Realities and Illusions of Power in the EU

David Galloway

★ UACES ★

www.SheffieldAcademicPress.com

Published by
Sheffield Academic Press Ltd
Mansion House
19 Kingfield Road
Sheffield S11 9AS
England

Typeset by Sheffield Academic Press
and
Printed on acid-free paper in Great Britain
by MPG Books Limited
Bodmin, Cornwall

British Library Cataloguing-in-Publication Data

A catalogue record for this book is available
from the British Library

ISBN 1-84127-271-X

Contents

Boxes

Tables

Foreword

Explaining EU treaties is a thankless task as any self-respecting politician or journalist will readily admit. This is especially true if, as in the case of the Treaty of Nice, the focus is EU institutional reform. Yet the Nice Intergovernmental Conference was much more than just a technocratic exercise. With the European Union on the verge of fulfilling its historical destiny by reaching out towards the continent's geographical limits, making sure its institutions can function while playing host to many more members concerns all of Europe's citizens, both inside the Union and in candidate states. The Treaty of Nice is a significant milestone down the road to enlargement; once it has been ratified, the Union will have fulfilled its commitment to be ready to welcome new members.

Although institutional reform may not feature high on most people's list of priorities, it is increasingly recognized that in an interdependent world our future can only be secured through cooperating in support of common objectives. Such cooperation is being articulated more and more through the Union's institutions and reaches into nearly every area of government, from foreign policy and external relations, including military and civilian crisis management, to economic policy coordination, internal security, global environmental problems, employment and the drive for economic competitiveness and social renewal in the new knowledge-based economy. If the Union's institutions are not up to the tasks that we entrust to them, it is not only the Union but every member state, and ultimately every citizen, that will feel the effects.

Having myself been closely involved in the Intergovernmental Conference, I know at first hand the complexities and difficult political choices heads of state and government were confronted with in Nice. Although the issues appeared deceptively simple, they concealed a complex nexus of problems relating to institutional efficiency which impinged on the power balance among member states in the Union. Not only has David Galloway captured the negotiations in all their complexity in this book, but he has managed to present the issues in a straightforward and accessible way. This is no mean feat. David's analysis of the politics underlying the decisions taken at Nice and his clear explanations of why the Nice summit reached the conclusions that it did make this book an invaluable resource for EU scholars and practitioners alike.

EU treaties have a habit of attracting criticism as soon as they have been negotiated. However, as for its predecessors, a dispassionate re-appraisal in the fullness of time will undoubtedly cast the Treaty of Nice in a more nuanced light. David's book is a timely and forward-looking contribution to that endeavour.

Javier Solana
Secretary-General
Council of the European Union
High Representative
for the CFSP

Brussels, March 2001

Series Foreword

Since the Treaty of Maastricht created the European Union, there have been two further efforts—the Amsterdam Treaty and the Nice Treaty— by the Union's member states to improve on the Maastricht model. The Treaty of Nice 2001 has been necessitated by the prospect of enlargement of the Union and the probability of the number of member states increasing by anything up to a dozen. Nice represents the current membership preparing the institutions and decision-making for life after enlargement.

Given that this series aims at providing authoritative texts on important aspects of European integration, we are indeed pleased to have David Galloway from the Secretariat of the Council of the European Union writing a book on the EU after the Nice Treaty. To echo the words of Javier Solana, he presents both the Nice negotiations and their consequences in 'a straightforward and accessible way'.

This book provides the background to the Nice Intergovernmental Conference (IGC) and then lays out in an understandable form the consequences of the treaty negotiated at Nice for EU institutions and decision-making. It examines these aspects of the Union in the shadow of enlargement.

At the start of 2001 it was decided that Jackie Gower would take over as Editor-in-Chief of the Contemporary European Studies series. I wish her all the best in that job. The editorial board will consist of Jackie, together with Judith Batt, Michael Newman, Stephen George and myself. Indeed, I would like to thank Jackie, Judith and Stephen for sharing the editorial duties for this book with me, and Javier Solana for providing a Foreword. Again, thanks are due to the staff of Sheffield Academic Press, especially Heidi Robbins, for making sure that this work is published so soon after the signing of the Nice Treaty on 26 February 2001.

Clive Archer
Editorial Board

Acknowledgments

This book owes its existence to the numerous friends, colleagues, journalists and academics who repeatedly asked me what had actually been agreed in the Treaty of Nice as they struggled to make sense of conflicting readouts of the December 2000 Nice summit. Whether the assessment in this book is any clearer will be for you, the reader, to judge.

Negotiating a treaty is very much a team effort. In writing this book I have drawn on conversations over the past year with many dedicated experts in national negotiating teams, the Commission and the European Parliament who are too numerous to thank individually. I would, however, like to express my appreciation to Jill Aussant, Jürgen Huber, Marta Arpio and Luis Teixeira da Costa in the Council Secretariat who offered helpful comments and suggestions on initial drafts. I would especially like to thank Jacques Keller-Noëllet whom I have been fortunate to have as my mentor since the 1996 Amsterdam IGC. Jacques' knowledge, experience and depth of insight as a result of being intimately involved in four IGCs and nearly sixty European Councils are second to none. Arguing through many of the issues raised in this book together with him during the Conference was always an intellectual challenge. His suggestions in clarifying and working through some of the concepts set out in Chapter 9, in particular Box 9.2, were extremely helpful. Andrea Laubengeiger, Lieve de Nil, Carina Berg and Donatella Mauri deserve a special mention for searching out documents, assisting with the layout and their guesswork in deciphering my scribbles. Thanks are also due to Monika Neumeister for compiling the index.

The fact that this manuscript was completed so promptly is entirely due to the tight deadlines imposed by Clive Archer which spurred me on in moments of flagging momentum. Clive, Judy Batt, Stephen George and Jackie Gower all provided useful suggestions and comments.

Finally and most importantly, I owe a debt of gratitude to my wife Kate and Beatrice, Ralph and Jamie who helped put the IGC in proper perspective. Just when they thought it was all over at Nice, their patience was tried for a further three months until this manuscript was completed. This book is dedicated to them.

The views or interpretations expressed in this book are my own and in no way commit the Council, any of its members or its General Secretariat. The usual culprit is to blame for any errors of fact or judgment.

David Galloway
Brussels, March 2001

Abbreviations

CAP	Common Agricultural Policy
CFI	Court of First Instance
CFSP	Common Foreign and Security Policy
COREPER	Permanent Representatives Committee
EC	European Community
ECB	European Central Bank
ECJ	European Court of Justice
ECSC	European Coal and Steel Community
ECOFIN	Economic and Finance Ministers' Council
EFC	Economic and Financial Committee
EIB	European Investment Bank
EMU	Economic and Monetary Union
EP	European Parliament
EU	European Union
Euratom	European Atomic Energy Community
Eurojust	European Judicial Co-operation Unit
ESDP	Common European Security and Defence Policy
IGC	Intergovernmental Conference
IIA	Interinstitutional Agreement
JHA	Justice and Home Affairs
MEDA	Measures to accompany econcomic and structural reforms in the framework of the Euro-Mediterranean partnership
MEP	Member of the European Parliament
NAFTA	North American Free Trade Area
NATO	North Atlantic Treaty Organization
QMV	Qualified Majority Voting
TACIS	Programme of Technical Assistance to the Commonwealth of Independent States
TEC	Treaty establishing the European Community
TEU	Treaty on European Union
WEU	Western European Union
WTO	World Trade Organization

1 |

Realities of Power in Today's European Union

Tocqueville sought the reasons for things in the things themselves
(Ampère).

The Treaty of Nice marks the completion of another renovation project
in the European Union (EU). It is designed to prepare the Union for the
biggest enlargement in its history by making the institutional changes
necessary for its membership to expand to 27 or more in the medium
term. The treaty has done no more and no less than that. Despite what
some commentators have claimed, it was never meant to do more;
conversely, failure would have had dire consequences on the timetable
for enlargement.

With the signature of the Treaty of Nice on 26 February 2001 almost
50 years to the day after the first founding treaty was signed in Paris on
18 April 1951, the Union has reached a watershed in its development.
The need for a clear blueprint for the future has never been more keenly
felt. Alongside the treaty, a Convention bringing together representatives of all national parliaments, the European Parliament, member state
governments and the Commission has drawn up a Charter of Fundamental Rights for the Union which was solemnly proclaimed at Nice.
European leaders have been vying with one another in offering a flurry
of new constitutional blueprints for the Union. President Chirac and
others have argued for a 'pioneer group' of member states to pull out of
the convoy into the fast lane and step on the accelerator of European
integration. The loosening up of the treaty provisions on so-called 'enhanced cooperation' (i.e. allowing a number of member states fewer
than the full membership to use the Union's institutions to move ahead
in certain policy areas) is viewed by some as a potential first step in that
direction. Accession negotiations with potential new member states are

continuing apace. Each of the Union's institutions is in the grips of far-reaching internal reforms. All of this activity has inevitably led some to conjure up the spectre of a European 'superstate', while others have lambasted the content of the Treaty of Nice for its lack of ambition and labelled it a failure.

Pity then the poor citizen trying to make sense of this hotchpotch. At a time in the Union's development when the need for clarity about its role and objectives has never been greater, confusing messages, not only about the Treaty of Nice but also about the broader debate on Europe, are only serving to heighten public mistrust. This mistrust is at least partly fuelled by the fact that the Union appears to be involved in an almost perpetual process of reform. The pace of change in recent years has been nothing short of breathtaking. Four major revisions of its founding treaties have been undertaken in the past fifteen years through a process of negotiation which goes under the somewhat cumbersome label of 'Intergovernmental Conference' (IGC). These IGCs led to the Single European Act (1986), the Treaty on European Union (the Maastricht Treaty) (1992), the Treaty of Amsterdam (1997) and now the Treaty of Nice (2001). Most of the previous treaty reform exercises inevitably raised broader questions about the scope of the Union's powers, the very nature of the European enterprise itself, and whether the institutions are sufficiently legitimate, accountable, democratic and transparent in the way that legislatures are expected to be in parliamentary democracies. While the Nice IGC deliberately refrained from tackling broader issues such as these, it has set in train a process beginning with a wide-ranging public debate on these questions in advance of a further revision of the Union's founding treaties scheduled for 2004.

Governing Today's European Union

From its beginnings in the 1950s, the European Union has grown to encompass fifteen member states and a population of more than 375 million inhabitants. Its geographical expansion from six founding member states has been matched by a significant extension of its powers, responsibilities and activities. People travelling across Europe now barely notice that they have crossed a national border. Consumer products must meet health and safety standards laid down in EU legislation. Businesses frame their manufacturing, marketing and merger strategies in the light of EU laws and regulations. Across most of the Union people will shortly have identical coins and notes in their pockets and wallets. The Union negotiates as a bloc in the World Trade Organization (WTO), and offers grants, loans, technical assistance and preferential access to its single market for developing countries. EU military and civilian crisis management capabilities are now in place. Whatever one's ideological standpoint on the European Union, its impact and reach are not in dispute. Virtually all government departments, national parliaments (albeit to varying degrees) and large sectors of civil society are involved to some extent in EU policy-making processes (see Dinan 1999; Nugent 1999).

Box 1.1: European Union and European Community

The terminology used to describe the Union/Community is confusing. There are three European Communities based on separate treaties: the European Coal and Steel Community (ECSC), the European Atomic Energy Community (Euratom) and the European Community (EC). By far the most important of these is the European Community. The ECSC Treaty expires in July 2002, and its tasks will then be subsumed into the European Community. The European Community is a legal order in which legislation is adopted through a legislative process and enforced by means of a judicial system based on member states' courts and the European Court of Justice which ensures uniform application and interpretation of the law.

The Treaty on European Union (the Maastricht Treaty) signed in 1992 established the European Union. The European Union is built around the existing European Communities and includes two additional *pillars*: the common foreign and security policy and cooperation in police and criminal justice matters. Although the Communities and the Union operate through a *single institutional framework* (i.e. Commission-Council-Parliament-Court), different decision-making modes exist under the second and third pillars (e.g. initiative right is not exclusively vested in the Commission and the European Parliament's role is more limited). Moreover, acts adopted under the second and third pillars are only justiciable in certain limited circumstances (extremely limited in the case of the second pillar).

The term European Union is often used as a generic name for both the Union and the Community and is used in this sense in this book, unless the legal distinction is relevant.

In all of these areas and a great many more besides, the Union passes laws and takes decisions that have legal effect in all member states and affect their citizens directly. This sets the Union aside from any other international grouping of states. It is able to do so because member governments, with the backing of national parliaments, have voluntarily pooled sovereign powers in carefully circumscribed areas and created institutions through which these collectively shared powers are exercised. This represents quite a radical departure from conventional views of sovereign power and is without precedent in modern times. Before the Second World War, the kind of Union we lived in was a pipedream other than in the minds of a few forward-looking visionaries. National sovereignty was deemed indivisible. Cooperation between states took place on the basis of shifting power bloc alliances for territorial or dynastic ends. Endowing the Union with a unique and carefully crafted institutional structure involving a balanced blend of supranational and intergovernmental features has undoubtedly been a key factor in its success. Its law-making institutions, including an indirectly elected Council of national government ministers and a directly elected European Parliament, co-decide most legislation. This legal order, upheld by an independent Court of Justice, is embodied in the various Treaties which are already acknowledged by the European Court of Justice to constitute a 'constitutional charter' (ECJ 1986).

Paradoxically, despite the inroads it has made into all its citizens' lives, the European Union has still largely failed to grip the public mind and imagination. Its institutions do not command the same allegiance nor evoke the same collective loyalty and passion as national and regional governments and parliaments. The low turnout for the 1999 European Parliament elections, which averaged 49.9% throughout the Union—and only 24% in the UK—is a worrying symptom of weak popular allegiance. The absence of a perceived common unifying heritage, tradition, 'myth' and a common destiny articulated through the Union's institutions, means that 'Brussels' is viewed as remote and detached from people's regional and national political culture, a place where rules and regulations are 'imposed' by faceless 'Eurocrats'. There are several understandable reasons for this perceived remoteness.

First, the Union's institutional architecture has no counterpart anywhere in the world. Although the Union's institutions perform similar functions to those carried out by a national legislature (parliament), executive (government) and judiciary (courts), these functions are not neatly separated in the way people have come to expect in a national context. Indeed, their design is so novel that portraying the working of the Union's main institutions by drawing direct analogies with institutional equivalents in a national context (with the possible exception of the Court of Justice) only serves to cloud understanding of the way in which the institutions function. Approaching the Union this way is arguably at least in part responsible for nurturing the misconception that the European Union is evolving towards some national institutional model and separation of powers.

Second, the Union is composed of fifteen national public opinions of very different cultural, religious and political traditions. One of the consequences of this is that politicians and national media tend to portray EU policy and law-making in terms of the domestic political arena. Most important policy decisions are taken by elected politicians in the shape of national government representatives in the Council of the European Union, with the European Parliament involved in many instances as co-legislator. However, ministers representing national governments in the Council are all too eager to claim 'positive' Union decisions as a national and personal triumph, while the blame for less favourable outcomes is placed squarely on the shoulder of 'Brussels' (i.e. the Union in general, and more often than not the Commission in particular). Even in the European Parliament, voting patterns frequently break down into national positions cutting across party political affiliations. Moreover, since policy decisions are often wrongly attributed to the Commission alone, it frequently becomes a scapegoat for decisions in reality taken by the Council and the European Parliament. This reinforces the popular misconception that most decisions are being taken by appointed public servants (i.e. the Commission) and not by elected political representatives in the Council, frequently acting in tandem with the European Parliament. Hence, the Union is all too often viewed by the public as some sort of extraneous entity rather than as part and parcel of the process of government involving their elected political representatives.

Third, the Union's increasing complexity, impinging on virtually every area of domestic policy, makes it difficult to apprehend the big picture and the fundamental political reasons behind the project. It is all too easy for the media, practitioners and politicians to fall into one of two extremes when characterizing the Union. The first is becoming too focused on procedural details of the mechanics of the system. The complexity of a factual description of the co-decision procedure used for adopting most EU legislation (which, incidentally, is simpler than legislative procedures in many national parliaments) fails to convey the politics of what is in reality a dynamic and politically charged negotiating process involving the European Parliament, the Council and the Commission. The second is lapsing into polemical caricatures of the outcome of policy decisions. Decisions on matters such as noise emissions of lawn mowers or what constitutes chocolate—both highly contentious political debates—can easily be made to look farcical if the serious economic, social and political issues underlying them are ignored. Both extremes fail to convey the dynamics of the political processes at work in and around the Union's institutions.

These broader questions go beyond the institutional reforms undertaken at the Nice IGC. However, the reform agenda over the coming years must respond to the problem of the Union's perceived remoteness if popular backing for the Union in general, and enlargement in particular, is to be enlisted and sustained in the long term. The point is that given the Union's pervasive impact in its citizens' daily lives as a layer of governance now firmly anchored in the political process in all member states (Peterson and Bomberg 1999), the way in which its institutions perform the tasks entrusted to them self-evidently matters. The negotiation of the Treaty of Nice and the renewed debate on Europe and its institutions are therefore anything but purely academic or technical exercises.

Understanding the Stakes of the Nice IGC

It was never the aim of the Nice IGC to undertake a wholesale revision of the Union's founding treaties. Its remit was clearly limited to streamlining the existing institutional structures 'so that the Union should be in a position to welcome new members from the end of 2002' (Council 1999e). Ostensibly the IGC's purpose was to deal with issues of efficiency in an enlarged Union; that is, what needed to be done so that the Union's institutions can function effectively with 27 or more member states. While a number of governments accordingly considered the IGC's priorities to be extending qualified majority voting (QMV) and making enhanced cooperation workable, since both would be instrumental in improving efficiency, efficiency in the minds of most was equated with preserving power and influence in an enlarged Union. Redistributing power inside the Union among the member states is always a fraught exercise, particularly when the scope for final endgame trade-offs is limited by a narrow agenda (see Chapter 2). Understanding the Treaty of Nice therefore requires an understanding of the politics behind the redistribution of power issues which dominated the Conference.

One way of approaching the power politics behind the Treaty of Nice is to consider different levels of 'equilibria' which can be found in the Union. Balance is a recurring theme in literature describing the workings of the Union—for example, 'balanced blend' of supranationalism and intergovernmentalism, the Union's 'institutional balance', an 'overall balanced outcome' to negotiations. It is hardly surprising therefore, that architecture, with its concerns for engineering stability and aesthetic equilibrium, provides one of the most common metaphorical crutches for describing the Union's structures and processes. Three layers of balance exist in the Union. Any constitutional change ultimately involves a dynamic shift in one or other of these power balances, each involving different players.

First of all, the *balance between the member states and the European Union*, which can be more accurately described as the constitutional share-out of powers between the Union/Community and the member states: that is, what the Union and the member states respectively can and cannot do. The treaties of course circumscribe the limits of Community action so the notion of equilibrium between the Community and the member states in a static sense is relatively unproblematic. The Community has a clear legal existence separate from the member states and can only act 'within the limits of the powers conferred' by the treaty (Article 5 TEC), thus debunking the myth that the Union can somehow acquire unlimited powers by its own institutions' actions. If need be, any grey areas can be clarified by the Court of Justice. More interesting, however, is the dynamic shift of this 'equilibrium' over time as successive treaty revisions have extended the Union's powers. Indeed, evolving towards 'ever closer Union' created a natural presumption in IGCs prior to Nice that powers should be extended and, between IGCs, at least in the Community's early days, that as broad an interpretation as possible should be followed in implementing the treaty. However, the logic of the 'Monnet method' (i.e. fostering political integration beginning by pooling sovereignty in a limited number of specific economic sectors and relying on gradual 'spillover' effects into new policy areas) has probably reached its limits with the transfer to the Union of certain core powers relating to economic and monetary union (EMU), foreign policy (CFSP) and internal security (JHA). Handling these core powers at Union level has meant devising new procedural approaches. Questions such as the extent to which these core powers in the latter two cases should be exercised by the Union, and, conversely, whether the Union might have gone too far in detailed regulation of certain economic and social areas, will·be at the forefront of the debate on the Union's future which was launched at Nice. However, as far as the Treaty of Nice itself was concerned, all negotiators were at pains to avoid any extension of the Union's and the Community's powers beyond their current limits in order to obviate the need for referendums in certain member states.

Second, the system of *checks and balances which operate between the Union's policy-making and legislative institutions* (the Commission, the Council and the European Parliament)—the so-called 'institutional triangle'. This 'institutional balance'—a term which is not without its critics (Wallace 2000)—is in reality a shifting, dynamic equilibrium which has evolved over time as the powers of certain institutions have increased with successive treaties—most notably those of the European Parliament—and as a result of subtle shifts in the ways the institutions interact and exploit their powers within the framework laid down in the treaties. The Conference shared a desire to carry out the changes required for enlargement without substantially altering existing institutional relationships. This was particularly evident in discussing certain issues relating to the Commission and the European Parliament (see Chapters 3 and 6 respectively).

Third, the *equilibrium within the Union among the member states themselves*; in other words how the Union reflects in its institutional structure the power balance between equally sovereign member states of very different sizes and levels of prosperity. The treaty explicitly mentions that the Union is an 'ever closer union among the peoples of Europe', though not a Union of member states. Nevertheless, Article 1 TEU states that the Union's tasks shall be 'to organise, in a manner demonstrating consistency and solidarity, relations between the Member states and between their peoples'. Article 6(3) TEU states that 'the Union shall respect the national identities of its Member states'. The Union, although it incontestably has a constitutional dimension, is a creation of treaties under international law, the contracting parties to which are the member states. The dual nature as a 'Union of states' and a 'Union of peoples' was one of the recurring themes in the negotiations, with negotiators placing greater emphasis on *peoples* or *states* depending on negotiating points being pressed as well as general perceptions of the nature of the Union. By focusing the Nice IGC agenda on the institutional changes necessary to accommodate new member states within the Union's existing institutional structure, issues of 'balance' among member states (i.e. their relative power and influence in the Union's institutions) inevitably featured prominently. It was power issues of this type that drove the Conference.

Therefore, underlying many of the 'size' issues lurked the question of 'presence' and influence in the Union's institutions. Indeed, three of the key political endgame issues reflected concerns of this type: the size and composition of the Commission, the weighting of votes in the Council and the allocation of seats in the European Parliament (see Chapters 3, 4 and 6 respectively). Similar issues arose in connection with the Court of Justice and the Court of Auditors (see Chapter 8). However much one may be critical of approaches which consider issues of size of the EU institutions in terms of member states' 'presence', given that member states are not 'represented' or even 'present' in the college of commissioners or the Court of Justice, this was the underlying political reality of the IGC negotiations. Even on enhanced co-operation, which was widely perceived as an efficiency issue, some of the most difficult sticking points related to balancing the respective rights and obligations of participating and non-participating member states (see Chapter 7).

Problems of governance in the European Union certainly extend well beyond the question of national presence in the institutions. However, it was never the Conference's intention to address broader issues affecting the power balance between the Union and the member states by extending Community or Union competence (see Chapter 5), nor to alter substantially the European Parliament-Council-Commission inter-institutional relationship. Misunderstandings on these counts by certain observers explain some of the initial criticism levelled at the Conference's apparent lack of ambition against a backdrop of visionary speeches by most of Europe's leaders throughout 2000.

Beyond Nice: The Future of the Union

With the preservation of peace as one of its primary founding aims, the Union's ultimate vocation to incorporate all European states is now heralded as an ever more distinct possibility. The combined impact of the Union's expansion in the medium term virtually to the geographical

limits of Europe coupled with a widely-held desire to avoid watering
down the integration process, are prompting a wider rethink of the
Union's institutional structure and its relationship with its member
states. At stake is how to tailor the Union to the future needs of extended membership while retaining broad public support and ensuring that
the Union remains a dynamic and cohesive unit. The need to improve
and monitor the democratic legitimacy and transparency of the Union
and its institutions is universally accepted. Neither an outright federalist
nor a wholly intergovernmental approach can offer a unifying vision for
designing a Union strong and stable enough to deal with the future
challenges confronting it. Chapter 9 outlines in more detail this debate
launched by Europe's leaders in 2000 and the parameters for carrying it
forward set out in the Nice declaration on the future of the Union
attached to the new treaty. The culmination of this process will be
another Intergovernmental Conference in 2004.

Aim of this Book

This book does not contain a detailed legal exegesis of treaty texts, but
analyses from a practitioner's viewpoint the fundamental political and
philosophical perceptions and choices underlying the Nice IGC. It
describes what has been agreed in the Treaty of Nice, and why, by:

- explaining the issues addressed during the IGC negotiations and
  analysing the practical impact of the changes to the Union's institutional structures agreed in the new treaty;
- offering an insight into the dynamics of the negotiating processes in
  the Intergovernmental Conference in achieving the political outcome accepted by all heads of government at Nice. Although it
  operates completely outside the Union's institutional framework,
  the IGC replicates a negotiating dynamic akin to that found in the
  Council of the European Union in which both the European Commission and the European Parliament are involved to varying
  degrees;
- placing the institutional reforms which have been agreed in the
  context of the wider debate about the Union which has engaged
  practically every European leader during 2000 and which formed a
  political undercurrent throughout the Conference's work.

In considering these questions, this book contends that the treaty has, with certain provisos, succeeded as a renovation job to ensure workable institutions for enlargement; that the Conference was largely about issues of power rather than issues of efficiency; that some of the criticism directed at the manner in which the treaty was negotiated has wrongly been misdirected at the content of the treaty; that alternative methods of preparing Intergovernmental Conferences merit being explored but cannot in themselves offer a panacea to the difficulties of agreeing constitutional change in the Union which will be faced by the 2004 IGC; and that the future IGC will necessarily focus essentially on the relationship between the member states and the Union, and, as a corollary, the 'balance' between its policy-making institutions, since issues of balance among the member states inside the Union's institutions have, for the most part, been laid to rest in the Treaty of Nice.

2 |

The Institutional Building Site

Since the mid-1980s, the Union has been involved in a rapid succession of major negotiations on treaty revision, medium-term financial frameworks and enlargements. Like history, this cycle is again repeating itself. With the successful conclusion of a new seven-year financial framework ('Agenda 2000') at the Berlin European Council in March 1999, the way was clear for the Union to launch a new IGC to tackle the institutional questions unresolved at Amsterdam in 1997 (the so-called 'Amsterdam leftovers') to remove the remaining stumbling block to enlargement inside the Union.

An IGC is the mechanism whereby EU member governments revise the Union's founding treaties. Although the Union's institutions are politically involved in this process to varying degrees, it is, formally speaking, a diplomatic negotiation among member governments, the outcome of which is enshrined in a treaty amending the existing treaties. These amendments enter into force once all fifteen member states have ratified them in accordance with their respective internal procedures, which either involve a parliamentary procedure or, in certain circumstances in some member states, a referendum. Under this process, which is very much in the realms of international treaty law, the member states remain the 'masters of the Treaties'. Criticism has, however, been levelled at the treaty revision process on the grounds that it should be both more *efficient* and more *legitimate*.

- The current methods for negotiating treaty change described in this chapter, have been criticized for being ill-suited to the negotiation of texts of legal and constitutional importance. First, the negotiating method, based on a four-tier vertical negotiating structure, suffers from structural weaknesses similar to those found in the Council. It is widely recognized that it is difficult for the Conference at ministerial level to exert any commanding authority over or make any significant input into the process, for the reasons explained below.

Second, achieving an acceptable outcome on difficult issues inevitably involves striking a political balance in the drafting of treaty language. Hence, the outcome occasionally suffers in terms of legal clarity and quality of drafting. More significantly, because texts are approved by heads of government, it is in practice impossible after the event to alter language which has received their blessing unless the changes are deemed unanimously to be of a purely legal and linguistic nature. Even apparently neutral changes suggested as part of this exercise, which every treaty undergoes before it is signed, do not always command universal approval and cannot therefore be taken on board. Various suggestions have been made for improving the process on both counts (McDonagh 1998). Over and above the question of whether the Conference should be preceded by a different kind of preparatory exercise than used on previous occasions (see Chapter 9), the fact that an IGC will in any case be held in 2004 (since Article 48 TEU has not been amended) means that serious consideration will need to be given to improving the efficiency of the IGC's working methods as part of the ongoing process of Council reform.

- The legitimacy of the process has also been challenged on two counts. First, given that the Union is much more than a conventional international organization and that the Treaties already have a constitutional dimension, many, including the European Parliament, consider that a broader based participation than national governments is required for negotiating treaty change. The Parliament, supported by a number of heads of government, has advocated that a body similar to the Convention used to negotiate the Charter of EU fundamental rights alongside the Nice IGC, and which was composed of representatives of national governments, national parliaments, the European Parliament and the Commission, should be used for preparatory work for the 2004 IGC. Moreover, the European Parliament has also stated that it would like to be directly involved at all negotiating levels in the IGC itself, and to have a right of assent over the final outcome. Second, some have argued that successive transfers of powers to the Union effected by previous treaty changes (though not at Nice) have resulted in a de facto extension in the discretion of national executives in the domestic arena at the expense of political control through national parliaments without any corresponding increase in parliamentary control at EU level (Lord 1998). They have consistently contended that, in addition to broader participation in the preparatory process, this warrants a greater degree of legitimation than that afforded by a simple 'take-it-or-leave-it' basis on which either national parliaments or electorates give their backing to their government's position.

The Conference's working methods came under renewed criticism on both counts immediately after Nice given the conditions in which heads of government reached a final agreement. The remainder of this chapter looks at how the preparatory and negotiating process of the Nice IGC was organized, before commenting further on these general points.

Setting the IGC Agenda

Launching an IGC is a cumbersome business involving intense political bargaining to fix a timeframe, determine a preliminary agenda and set in train the preparatory phase of work. Following this political preparatory phase, the process of formally convening the Conference is relatively straightforward. After that, negotiating begins in earnest and presidencies (i.e. national governments holding the six-month rotating presidency of the Council of the European Union) are confronted with the difficult task of organizing the agenda, managing the negotiating process and steering it to a successful conclusion. The Nice IGC followed the well-established pattern.

This time round the Conference was not beginning with a clean slate. The origins of the Nice IGC lie in the protocol on the institutions with the prospect of enlargement annexed to the treaties at the end of the Amsterdam IGC in 1997 (see Box 2.1). During that IGC, the need to resolve the difficult institutional issues for enlargement was less pressing: at that time enlargement was still a remote prospect and no decisions had been taken to open accession negotiation with any candidate states. Thus Amsterdam avoided the key institutional issues and member governments undertook to resolve the so-called 'Amsterdam leftovers' before enlargement. The foundation stone for the Nice IGC was laid at the Cologne European Council in June 1999 which agreed a timeframe for work, a preliminary list of topics to be addressed, and how the Conference should be prepared.

Box 2.1: Amsterdam protocol on the institutions with the prospect of enlargement

---

Article 1

At the date of entry into force of the first enlargement of the Union, notwith-standing Article 213(1) of the Treaty establishing the European Community, Article 23(1) of the Treaty establishing the European Coal and Steel Community and Article 149(1) of the Treaty establishing the European Atomic Energy Community, the Commission shall comprise one national of each of the Member states, provided that, by that date, the weighting of the votes in the Council has been modified, whether by re-weighting of the votes or by dual majority, in a manner acceptable to all Member states, taking into account all relevant elements, notably compensating those Member states which give up the possibility of nominating a second member of the Commission.

Article 2

At least one year before the membership of the European Union exceeds twenty, a conference of representatives of the governments of the Member states shall be convened in order to carry out a comprehensive review of the provisions of the Treaties on the composition and functioning of the institutions.

Timing

The need to complete the IGC by the end of 2000 was readily agreed. If the Union was serious in its political commitment to be ready to accommodate new member states from the end of 2002, the Conference would have to wind up by the end of 2000 at the latest and the new treaty signed in early 2001 given the likely need for at least an eighteen month ratification period. With the fairly narrow agenda envisaged for the Nice IGC, this timetable was quite feasible.

Scope of the Agenda

Finding language to define the scope of the Conference's agenda proved more problematic. While Article 1 of the protocol on the institutions only specifically mentioned two issues (the size and composition of the Commission and the weighting of votes in the Council), Article 2 foresaw the possibility of a 'comprehensive review of the operation and functioning of the institutions'. In addition, the final act of the Amsterdam Treaty contained a declaration by the Conference relating to the special situation of Spain (see Chapter 5), as well as a trilateral declaration by Belgium, France and Italy regarding the scope of qualified majority voting which stated that 'a significant extension of recourse to qualified majority voting forms part of the relevant factors which should be taken into account' under the treaty protocol. Despite the shared starting premise that the Union should only undertake reforms necessary for enlargement, views on precisely what those reforms should be differed profoundly due to different political perceptions of the stakes. Advocates of a minimalist agenda were sensitive to the need to avoid opening up a disruptive debate on the fundamental nature of the European Union, particularly at a time that might be counter-productive for British participation in the single currency. It was also feared that an expanding agenda might put in jeopardy the planned timetable for the Conference with knock-on effects for enlargement negotiations. Maximalists argued on the other hand that since radical reforms would be required to ensure that a Union of 27-plus member states could function effectively, the Conference should take full advantage of the fact that this would probably be the last opportunity to make such substantial changes before enlargement.

As a result of the decisions taken at the Luxembourg and Helsinki European Councils, the Union had in the meantime opened negotiations with twelve candidate states and accorded the status of candidate state to Turkey. A further potential agenda-setting issue therefore was whether the Conference was operating in the framework of Article 1 or Article 2 of the Protocol. Article 1 described a situation in a Union of up to twenty member states and also provided for a trade-off between large member states relinquishing the right to nominate a second commissioner and Council vote weighting. Article 2 called for a comprehensive review of the composition and functioning of the institutions in a Union of more than twenty members. In the end, however, no attempts were made to use the protocol as a procedural device for manipulating the Conference agenda.

The topics singled out at the Cologne European Council in June 1999 were confirmed in the mandate agreed at the Helsinki European Council in December of the same year. This mandate left sufficient leeway for the Conference to cover institutional reforms for enlargement in a broad sense. Helsinki listed three specific agenda items: the size and composition of the Commission, the weighting of votes in the Council, and the *possible* extension (emphasis added) of qualified majority voting. The Helsinki conclusions also stated that the Conference would consider 'other necessary treaty amendments regarding the institutions in connection with these issues and in implementing the Treaty of Amsterdam', and agreed that the incoming presidency should report to the European Council on progress in the Conference and 'may propose additional issues to be taken on the agenda' (Council 1999e).

This preliminary skirmishing and tactical positioning was at least partly inspired by the idea that setting a wide or a narrow agenda in the European Council conclusions before the start of the IGC would pin it down once and for all. Although no agreement existed on the specific subjects to be addressed, all parties shared a starting premise that the Conference should only undertake institutional changes necessary for enlargement. In such circumstances, investing effort in trying to establish a clear mandate was likely to be unproductive for two reasons: first, attempts to reconcile minimalists and maximalists would result in precisely the sort of compromise that emerged from Helsinki; and second, provided all participants were operating within a commonly accepted overarching framework, the agenda would tend to evolve naturally to encompass the range of subjects that were generally acknowledged to need addressing. Unforeseen external events also forced subjects onto the agenda. The formation of a government coalition in Austria including the far right Freedom Party and the subsequent sanctions imposed by fourteen member governments focused particular attention on Article 7 TEU relating to violations of fundamental rights by a member government. This prompted a wider debate of this issue in the context of enlargement, in particular the need for an early warning procedure in the event of a risk of such a violation. At the end of the day, apart from establishing a broad framework for work, attempts to fix precisely an agenda in a relatively narrowly defined exercise of this type generally represent an inefficient expenditure of time and effort. The agenda is ultimately determined at the end of work by the content of the final treaty!

Preparatory Work Ahead of the IGC
Aside from agenda setting, getting an IGC off the ground normally involves a political preparatory exercise. Three options existed for preparing the Nice IGC. The first would be to constitute a 'wise persons' group composed of a limited number of experts or political personalities. While this method offers the prospect of a coherent report on the issues to be handled, such an arrangement runs the risk of being too detached from the political reality of an IGC as perceived by member

state governments. The second is to set up a group of fifteen national representatives, plus representatives of the Commission and the European Parliament, to draw up an annotated agenda. However, any such 'negotiated' preparatory report is inevitably of limited usefulness since it tends to result in a national position-based rather than an issue-based document in which participants stake out their opening bids for the Conference. Unlike in the run-up to the Amsterdam IGC where precisely such an approach was followed with the Westendorp Group, the Cologne European Council opted for a third approach by inviting the Finnish presidency to draw up on its own responsibility a report 'explaining and taking stock of options for resolving the issues to be settled' (Council 1999c). This would avoid pre-negotiating among fifteen governments a series of highly politically contentious issues with the attendant risk of rigidifying positions at an early stage. Moreover, it afforded the presidency a free hand to produce a report which could take a more analytical look at the avenues to be explored by the Conference rather than merely collating fifteen different viewpoints. All of these possibilities ultimately leave the process under the firm grip of national governments, since even in the event of selecting 'wise persons', their 'wisdom' would be determined by national governments selecting them.

The Finnish presidency began by undertaking a series of formal and informal consultations with Permanent Representatives (i.e. each member state's Ambassador to the EU), the Commission and the European Parliament. After having sought on its own initiative a contribution from three 'wise men' (Dehaene *et al.* 1999), the Commission offered a written contribution to the preparatory work (European Commission 1999) which prefigured the detailed opinion it would subsequently present at the launch of the Conference. In the light of sensitivities about the agenda, the presidency elected to produce a brief report (Council 1999d) reflecting the prevailing mood of delegations on the key questions rather than undertaking a detailed analysis of these issues at this early stage. Given the underlying philosophical disagreement on the scope of the Conference, this strategy proved to be a safe option. The report identified a number of issues which would need to be addressed in addition to the three explicitly mentioned in the Cologne conclusions, such as the allocation of seats in the European Parliament and legislative procedures, the Court of Justice and Court of First Instance, the Court of Auditors, and other Union bodies. Though the issue of enhanced cooperation was raised at this stage of work and strongly advocated by some as a topic for the IGC, the report echoed the widespread view at that time that the Conference should not consider this issue on its agenda. There was one issue (QMV) where the presidency report made a particularly useful contribution to the Conference's work by outlining a methodology for categorizing groups of articles which was taken up by the Portuguese presidency as a basis for work on QMV during the first half of 2000.

The presidency's report was welcomed by the Helsinki European Council. However, in the face of strong insistence that discussion of enhanced cooperation should not be definitively excluded from future work (see Chapter 7), the European Council left open a window for the presidency to 'propose additional issues to be taken on the agenda of the Conference' (Council 1999e) in the report to be made to the Feira European Council in June.

Formally Convening the Conference

With the political foundations in place at Helsinki, the necessary procedural steps could then be taken to convene the Conference officially. The formal procedure is laid down in Article 48 TEU and involves four steps, which are described in Box 2.2.

Actors in the Conference

Member States

Once the Conference has been launched, the institutions themselves no longer have any formal role to play in negotiating and adopting the outcome. Even though the Conference is convened by the member state exercising the presidency of the Council, the Council itself has no institutional role. Notwithstanding this fact, and the fact that the European Parliament had two observers at all of the Conference's Preparatory Group meetings, the European Parliament nevertheless tabled eighteen questions to the Council about the Conference! Negotiation takes place among EU member governments, since the 'constituent power' for treaty change lies with the member states as contracting parties to the treaties.

Box 2.2: Procedure for convening an IGC

Convening the Nice IGC involved four stages:

1. A *proposal* is required from a member state government or the Commission. Given that the European Council had already agreed in principle to the Conference, the Finnish government submitted a formal proposal for amending the Treaties on 13 December 1999 couched in language identical to the substantive part of the Helsinki European Council conclusions.

2. The Council must then *consult both the European Parliament and the Commission*, which it did on 17 December. The Commission issued a favourable opinion on 26 January 2000 along with a comprehensive communication setting out its detailed position on the matters which it considered the Conference should address. The European Parliament, after some hesitation due to dissatisfaction about the Parliament's role in the Conference (even though it represented a step forward compared to Amsterdam) as well as concerns about the Conference's overall lack of ambition, finally issued its opinion on 3 February 2000 along with a resolution setting out its position. The treaty also provides for the ECB to be consulted on institutional changes in the monetary area. Since it was impossible to predict at the outset whether any such changes would be made, the Bank was only consulted at the very end of the Conference once it became clear that amendments would be made to Articles 111(4) and 123(4) TEC, as well as Article 10 of the ECB statute.

3. The *Council* itself must then issue a *favourable opinion*, which it duly did on 13 February 2000. This was a purely formal act, since the Council does not attempt to reconcile its members' views given that the substance is negotiated among member governments in the Conference rather than in the Council;

4. The first session of the Conference is then *convened* by the presidency. This took place on 14 February 2000 and in line with established tradition was held at ministerial level.

The vertical negotiating structure of the Conference mirrored that found in the Council and met at four different levels (see Box 2.3). Two details are worth noting. Unlike previous Conferences, the Helsinki European Council conclusions expressly indicated that member state governments would be represented at ministerial level by 'Ministers who are members of the General Affairs Council' rather than 'foreign ministers'. While members of the General Affairs Council are indeed foreign ministers, this wording emphasized the fact that the General Affairs Council has a remit which covers much more than external relations. Second, representatives who undertook most of the detailed IGC work in the Preparatory Group were to act as representatives of their respective governments rather than simply their foreign ministers. The purpose was twofold: given the fact that the Conference's work cut across the full range of the Union's activities (see, for example, Appendix 2 which lists the areas where qualified majority voting has been extended) representatives had to articulate the interests of their governments rather than those of a particular government department. Second, ministers in the General Affairs Council are supposed to exercise a coordinating role for the work of the European Council, and should therefore play a similar role in the IGC in acting as a political filter for issues being channelled to heads of government.

Most member states (apart from Portugal, Germany, Spain, Ireland and Greece) were represented in the Preparatory Group by their Permanent Representatives to the European Union, thereby preserving overall homogeneity and peer group affinity. This was significant given the fact that this group shouldered the bulk of the preparatory work and in view of the limited contribution that General Affairs Ministers were able to make. Like at Amsterdam, ministers experienced difficulty in carving out a satisfactory role in the negotiations, given that for the most part they had little time or inclination to deal with IGC issues in depth. As a result, ministers found themselves 'squeezed' between heads of government who would ultimately take the key political decisions, and the Preparatory Group undertaking the detailed 'technical' work on these political issues.

The Presidency
The presidency acts as the engine driving the Conference by setting the overall pace of work, planning and organizing the agenda, producing discussion papers and brokering compromises. While other member states, the Commission and the European Parliament produce papers setting out their positions in general terms or on specific points, it is the presidency working papers which constitute the negotiating basis for the Conference. The presidency's role is neatly encapsulated in this description from the Amsterdam IGC:

> A presidency cannot invent a way forward out of thin air. It must, at the same time, guide and shape the direction of the Conference. It is not a scissors and paste job. Defining the real underlying agenda—identifying the European interest, recognising what will run and what will not, developing language that will be both effective and acceptable—is a complex and subtle challenge. It is an art form rather than a science. (McDonagh 1998).

Box 2.3: Organization of the Nice Intergovernmental Conference

The Conference's work was organized at four levels:

1. *Heads of state or government* who were responsible for taking the final political decisions. Heads of government discussed the IGC at Feira in June and more substantively at the informal European Council in Biarritz in October, where some frank exchanges on the key political topics during a day and a half of discussions on the IGC ultimately marked a turning point in preparing the final negotiating stage. The Nice heads of government meeting finished after 4.00 am on Monday 11 December 2000 after a marathon four-day session (the longest ever for a summit, although not all of which was devoted to the IGC).

2. *Ministers in the General Affairs Council* had overall political responsibility for the Conference. During the French presidency, a number of meetings were also organized as informal ministerial Conclaves chaired by Pierre Moscovici, Minister for European Affairs. In practice, however, like at Amsterdam, ministers found themselves squeezed between the Preparatory Group where most of the detailed spadework was carried out, and heads of government, who alone carried the authority needed to take the necessary political decisions. Given the nature of the subject matter, the multiple issue interlinkages which tended to rule out partial agreements along the way, the relative infrequency of their meetings and not least because, with some exceptions, ministers showed little enthusiasm for subjects which lay outside their normal remits, it was difficult for them to assert commanding authority over the work of the Conference.

3. The *Preparatory Group,* made up of a representative of each member state's government, which carried out the detailed analytical work on the texts. Most of the representatives were their respective member states' Permanent Representative in Brussels (in ten cases), three were senior civil servants from their foreign ministries, and two member states were represented at junior ministerial level (Portugal and Germany). The group was chaired by Francisco Seixas da Costa until 30 June, then by Pierre Vimont.

4. Finally, the *Friends of the Presidency* group. This group consisted of a representative from each member state (Legal Counsellors) and was mandated by the Preparatory Group to undertake detailed technical work on revising the treaty articles and protocols on the Court of Justice and the Court of First Instance. This freed up more time for the Preparatory Group to concentrate on other issues, and proved to be a successful method for handling these more technical issues, since no questions relating to the Court were left outstanding for heads of government.

The Conference involved an estimated 350 hours of meetings at all levels over a ten-month period.

Preparatory Group meetings were convened on average around once a fortnight. The presidency had to pitch the content of its papers carefully. It had to ensure that they enabled delegations to enter into a genuine debate, without exposing itself needlessly to criticism by biasing or misrepresenting views on sensitive points. Following discussions, it was up to the presidency to assess how far to go in taking on board amendments to its drafts in the light of discussions. A great deal of discretion was left to the presidency in framing its papers. Since most debates took the form of a table round, with each delegation expressing its position, the presidency usually enjoyed considerable leeway to sum up in general terms and reflect after the meeting on the extent to which amendments should be taken on board in the next generation paper. These papers, which initially took the form of oriented questionnaires, over a period of months gradually acquired the form of draft treaty language by a process of successive approximation tending towards a point of equilibrium which all delegations would be likely to live with as part of the overall agreement.

While the practice of table round discussions makes it difficult to avoid repetition of stated positions, it generally proved to be a reasonably effective, albeit laborious, process which ensured that draft treaty language was given meticulous consideration. In addition to formal meetings, the presidency also engaged in detailed bilateral discussions with delegations as the Conference approached the critical end of presidency stage either to assist it in assessing the overall balance of the content of its interim report, or gauging strategy for end-game compromises.

The Portuguese presidency's task was to cover all the ground on the main topics and draw up a realistically ambitious report reflecting the state of play which would help ensure a smooth transition to the French presidency. A two-part report was presented to the Feira European Council that reflected the range of views and positions expressed by delegations and set out the presidency's evaluation of the state of play of the negotiations in the form of draft articles, illustrative tables and indicative lists (IGC 2000c). This approach offered three advantages: it left all options open, which was politically necessary at that stage; it indicated some of the more promising avenues for further work on certain issues; and it avoided lengthy conclusions on the IGC at the June Feira European Council which were neither desirable nor necessary.

The report bequeathed the French presidency a good starting basis on which to build.

The same working methods were followed throughout the French presidency until a summary document representing a first outline of the content of the treaty was produced for an informal Preparatory Group meeting in Paris on 3 November. This document was shaped over the coming four weeks into the draft treaty that was submitted to the Nice European Council.

The French presidency's task was complicated by a number of domestic factors. The internal coordination difficulties as a result of a socialist Prime Minister, Lionel Jospin, cohabiting with a conservative President, Jacques Chirac, had repercussions on the Conference's work, even though at Nice both worked closely together to strike the final agreement. France also had specific national difficulties on two key QMV issues before the Conference (on visas, asylum and immigration and on the common commercial policy). Moreover, the robust style adopted by the presidency at ministerial level on certain issues, particularly on the size and composition of the Commission, generated tensions which persisted throughout the latter half of the Conference. Some Conference participants felt that these factors led to shortcomings in the presidency's leadership, objectivity and efficiency. There was, however, a stark contrast between both the style and the careful and meticulous management of the process at Preparatory Group level which secured a well-prepared basis for heads of government, and a lack of strategic direction which some commentators claimed characterized part of the endgame negotiations, particularly on Council vote weighting (Ludlow 2001).

The European Commission
The Commission, given its particular role as independent guardian of the treaties, and by virtue of the fact that Article 48 TEU gives it the right to table proposals, participates at all levels of the Conference. The Commission, through its detailed opinion, formal and informal contributions and interventions in meetings, was an active participant throughout the Conference. It was represented by Michel Barnier, who had in fact been the French government representative during the Amsterdam IGC, and by President Prodi himself at heads of government level. The Commission can be a useful ally for the presidency, since its backing for presidency suggestions can help enlist support for

emerging compromises. In some respects it can almost be considered a sixteenth member state at the table, often representing a voice of ambition (albeit with varying degrees of realism) in the collective interest of the Union.

The Commission's prime concern throughout the Conference was to ensure that the Union decision-making would function as effectively as possible after enlargement. However, its impact was limited and it was involved to a much lesser extent than in normal Community business in the process of elaborating compromise proposals. There are three main reasons for this: the first is that while the president of the Commission is a fully-fledged sixteenth member of the European Council (which has acquired increasing pre-eminence in recent years as the helm of the Union's system of government), when heads of government are meeting in an IGC configuration the Commission is in a much weaker institutional and political position by virtue of the fact that it is not a member state government and therefore not formally part of the Conference. Under the treaty, however, the Commission has the right, alongside member governments, to make proposals for amending the treaties. The second was that on a number of politically high-profile areas where it had taken a strong public stance, such as seeking a significant extension of QMV on taxation, social security and social policy, and pleading strongly for a simple dual majority voting system (see Chapter 5), the Commission was defending politically difficult positions. Third, on the one issue of direct relevance to the Commission itself, namely its size, it crucially failed to take a clear stance.

The European Parliament
Over the years, the Parliament's role in successive IGCs has been a matter of controversy. Article 48 TEU gives the European Parliament no role whatsoever in the IGC itself, either to submit proposals or attend sessions of the Conference, nor does the Parliament have any formal role at the end of the process. The terms in which Article 48 is framed provide the basis for distinguishing between the Commission's and the European Parliament's role in the Conference.

Until the present IGC, the European Parliament had no formal representation at any of the Conference's meetings. During the Amsterdam IGC, due to French and UK opposition a rather baroque arrangement was put in place under which two European Parliament representatives would have additional meetings with IGC representatives, plus at least one informal dinner per month. This time round, however, the Helsinki European Council agreed that two 'observers' from the European Parliament may attend meetings of the Preparatory Group, but not formal ministerial meetings nor meetings of heads of government. During the Conference, this arrangement was also extended to Friends of the Presidency meetings and informal ministerial conclaves. This allowed the two observers (Elmar Brok, European Peoples Party, Germany; and Dimitrios Tsatsos, Party of European Socialists, Greece) to present the Parliament's position and argue on specific points of direct interest to the European Parliament (European Parliament 2000). Each formal ministerial session of the Conference was also preceded by an exchange of views with Nicole Fontaine, the president of the European Parliament, which was generally more stage-managed and formal in character. The Nice arrangements still fell short of the Parliament's call for the right to be a fully-fledged participant at all levels of the Conference, and to give its assent to the outcome.

Given the mismatch between the Parliament's initial ambitions for the Nice IGC, and the remit actually agreed by heads of government, it was predictable that whatever the Conference's outcome, the overall level of ambition would not satisfy the European Parliament. While the Parliament offers its assessment of the Conference by adopting a resolution at the end of its work, this is not a formal requirement for adopting the new treaty, although it sends a signal to national parliaments engaged in the ratification process (Jacobs 2000). The Parliament has hinted that it may delay adopting such a resolution pending the outcome of the Brussels European Council in December 2001 which will decide on appropriate initiatives for continuing the preparatory process for the next IGC in 2004, in which the Parliament expects to be closely involved.

The Conference Secretariat
The Council Secretariat acts as the secretariat for the Conference at the behest of the European Council. In theory, heads of government could designate whomsoever they choose to act as the Conference Secretariat, but given the fact that the logistics, negotiating style and compromise building process follow established patterns of negotiation within the Council, including similar vertical negotiating structures and largely the same players (see Box 2.3), the Council Secretariat is best equipped to fulfil that function. Apart from the Secretary-General/High Representa-

tive, Javier Solana, and the Deputy Secretary-General, Pierre de Boissieu, the Conference was in fact serviced by a small team of five 'A' grade officials, plus secretarial and linguistic backup, including the director for general policy questions in the Secretary-General's private staff and the director-general of the legal service acting as Legal Adviser to the Conference. The secretariat's job is to assist the Conference by offering its counsel to the presidency, producing initial drafts of documents as input for the presidency and acting as an informal backroom operator using its good offices in the interests of a successful outcome. In doing so, it was able to draw on the extensive experience it had acquired in the three most recent Intergovernmental Conferences prior to Nice.

Improving the Conference's Preparatory and Working Methods

The structures and negotiating methods of the Nice IGC replicated those followed during the Amsterdam IGC. No major innovations were introduced, other than allowing European Parliament observers to attend and intervene in all IGC debates at the Preparatory Group level, thereby affording it a bigger say than it had had in any previous IGC. Criticism of the Conference's working methods has, however, inevitably been followed by calls for a radical overhaul of the process of negotiating treaty change before the next treaty revision exercise scheduled for 2004.

This chapter has shown that the Conference's working methods, like those of the Council, have both strengths and weaknesses. The preparation at official level is thorough and meticulous, with most of the ramifications of treaty changes being carefully sifted and honed by experts who are close to their political masters. All government representatives and their respective negotiating teams were eminently qualified for the job and undertook their duties with professionalism and intellectual rigour. But no matter how good they were, Representatives in the Preparatory Group, with some exceptions, were not ministers empowered to make political choices. The task of preparing options for heads of government should have fallen to the General Affairs ministers. However, foreign ministers, as during the Amsterdam IGC, had difficulty squaring up to the task. The subjects handled by an IGC require a degree of specialist knowledge which goes beyond the remit of foreign ministers, for whom foreign affairs is the primary national centre of interest. This is likely to be equally true in the future IGC in 2004. Given recent advances in ESDP, it would appear to be placing unreasonable demands on foreign ministers to continue to ask them to maintain a high level of political expertise in the Union's major internal policies and institutional questions—which they need to possess if they are ever to assume an effective political leadership role in coordinating not only IGCs, but also the bulk of the subject matter channelled up to European Councils relating to EU internal policies. This raises more fundamental questions about the internal structure of the Council which go beyond the organizational arrangements for Intergovernmental Conferences, in particular the implications of establishing an appropriate ministerial forum as part of the ongoing process of Council reform (see Council 1999a).

At Amsterdam, heads of government suffered from a problem of overload with close on twenty major points of negotiation (some of them legally technical and complex) left open for resolution in the space of three days. At Nice the agenda was less wide ranging, but heads of government were again faced with overload on account of the depth of technical detail they were expected to get to grips with, particularly on Council vote weighting and certain aspects of qualified majority voting. In both cases, this suggests that an effective political filter below heads of government level to set out political choices is lacking. The result is over-reliance on a limited number of heads of government meetings (such as Biarritz and Nice) for crucial decisions to be taken. Inevitably, these meetings become political occasions of high drama under the intense gaze of the world's media at which the pace of negotiation picks up to almost breakneck speed. In the end, compromises need to be struck in difficult political circumstances which might not be the ideal outcome for some (or even many) participants. While caution needs to be exercised if changes are to be made to a system which has succeeded in bringing the Union to where it is today, there are evident shortcomings to be addressed in the way texts of a constitutional nature are negotiated.

The legitimacy of heads of government is unquestioned; they are the supreme political authority in the Union and are all democratically elected in each of their member states. The fact that their quarterly gatherings in the European Council attract on average more than 2000 journalists and that their political decisions are generally respected and followed up are adequate testimony to that. However, there appears to be a growing sense that the political preparatory process for treaty reform requires a broader based participation than it currently has. Heads of government themselves accept the need for broader participation in the preparatory process. The declaration on the future of the Union attached to the Nice final act calls for 'a deeper and wider debate about the future of the European Union' with the Swedish and Belgian presidencies, in cooperation with the Commission and involving the European Parliament, to encourage 'discussions with all interested parties; representatives of national parliaments and all those reflecting public opinion; political, economic and university circles, representatives of civil society, etc.'. However, broadening participation in the preparatory process which precedes an IGC, while probably a welcome and politically necessary move, is not in itself a guarantee of success. Chapter 9 considers this point in more detail.

3 |

The European Commission

In its conception the European Commission is the most original of the Union's institutions. Although it is not by any stretch of the imagination the 'government of Europe', nor even the Union's sole executive branch, it fulfils a vital and unique institutional role. It is guardian of the treaties and is required to act completely independently in representing and advancing the general interest; as such it has a right of initiative which is exclusive in Community matters and shared in other areas. In addition to being a policy initiator and developer, its duties include that of manager, enforcer, mediator and negotiator. It often acts as the Community's representative and speaks on its behalf in international negotiations. Given its special institutional role and the diversity of its functions, it is unquestionably in the interest of the Union as a whole, and of every member state, to have a strong, dynamic and effective Commission at the heart of the institutional structure.

The IGC had to address how the Commission should be composed, structured and organized in future in order to operate effectively after enlargement. The debate focused on three specific questions: the institution's size (i.e. the optimum number of commissioners), its internal organizational structure and the powers of its president, and issues relating to the individual or collective political accountability of commissioners. The first two were linked; the larger the Commission, the greater the need to foresee treaty provisions on its internal organizational structure. Much of the argument on these issues revolved around three underlying principles which were constantly restated in arguments advanced by both proponents and opponents of different approaches for organizing the Commission.

The first was *independence*. The Commission's independence depends first and foremost on the personal qualities and calibre of its members and its staff. It is an essential requirement if the Commission is to act effectively and credibly in the interest of the Union as a whole rather than any one member state, which is why the treaty sets such great store by it. Commissioners are not there to 'represent' the government of the member state they come from. Commissioners must be selected 'on the grounds of their general competence' as persons 'whose independence is beyond doubt'. They 'shall be completely independent in the performance of their duties' in the general interest and shall neither 'seek nor take instructions from any government or from any other body'. Member states have also undertaken to respect this principle and 'not to seek to influence members of the Commission in the performance of their tasks' (Article 213 TEC). In general the principles of independence and impartiality are respected. There are naturally sometimes suspicions that a particular commissioner or official has used his/her position to look sympathetically at a matter concerning his/her country, but this is not common (Nugent 2001). Although independent, the Commission does not propose in a vacuum. The Council, the European Parliament, Council presidencies, member states or pressure groups may urge the Commission to exercise its discretion, but cannot compel it to make a proposal. Before formalizing a proposal, particularly where important economic interests are at stake, the Commission usually undertakes a process of formal and informal consultation involving interested parties (industry, lobbies, interest groups), national governments, specialized agencies and its internal services. It may also consult the Council or the European Parliament as such by issuing communications or white papers to test the ground before putting forward formal proposals into the legislative process. It, of course, likes to make credible proposals which have a realistic chance of getting through the legislative mill without substantial watering down of any of the fundamental features which it considers best balance the often conflicting national and sectoral interests at stake. It is not unheard of for a final compromise on a particular directive to be achieved after months or years of deliberation exploring different avenues for a solution by reverting in substance to the original Commission proposal. Finding solutions in the IGC that ensured the Commission's independence would be crucial for preserving the credibility and political authority of the Commission in future.

Second, the *legitimacy* of the Commission's output. This derives primarily from the fact that its members are bound by the principle of collective responsibility and are accountable as a college to the European Parliament. Operating as a college subject to collective responsibility is vital for the legitimacy of its decisions as the Commission is neither an elected nor an intergovernmental body. The commissioners (including the president) are appointed collectively as a body and not on an individual basis; the Council and the Parliament cannot pick and choose individual appointees. All important and controversial decisions are prepared with the involvement of all commissioners who must bear collective responsibility for them and defend them as the Commission's view once they have been adopted by the college. Collegiality is also designed to ensure that action is taken in the general interest. Nugent points out that

> no commissioner can, without risk of being rebuked and possibly public-ly humiliated by colleagues, attempt to be too independent in public especially after the college has taken a decision on a matter. Commis-sioners are assigned individual policy responsibilities and are delegated certain decision-making powers but these are within carefully demarca-ted parameters. Within the parameters, commissioners must still always formally act under the name of the Commission rather than in an individual capacity (Nugent 2001).

However, collegiality requires cohesiveness. As the Commission has pointed out (European Commission 2000a), in the case of national governments, cohesiveness comes from having a shared political affil-iation or coalition interests backed by a parliamentary majority enabling them to implement a political programme. This is why national govern-ments can have as many ministers as they like without their ability to act being compromised. Given that the Union's institutional setup differs considerably from national systems of government, other means have to be found in order to preserve the Commission's cohesiveness. While a Commission limited in size might be one way of strengthening collegiality and legitimacy, many delegations equated legitimacy with the public 'acceptability' of the college's output. In their view this meant that the Commission should not only be seen to be taking account of all national interests in defining the general interest, but that a recognizable political 'face' inside the Commission of the same nationality should be available to state the Union's case in public politi-cal debate in each member state, particularly where unpopular decisions are involved.

Finally, the Commission's *effectiveness* of operation. No one dispu-ted the fact that efficiency and dynamism in the Commission will be vital to help secure its cohesion after enlargement. As the Commission itself observed in its opinion on the IGC: 'managing collective responsibility within a twenty member Commission already slows proceedings down in certain respects...and makes for a heavy administrative workload. The Commission takes thousands of decisions each year, some 200 or so each week' (European Commission 2000a). The issue was again size, but also the extent to which it might be necessary to sketch out in the treaty a particular structure for the Commission, without being over-prescriptive in limiting the Commission's and its president's discretion in putting in place organizational structures for optimum effectiveness. Improved administrative efficiency depends not only on the structures laid down in the treaty but also on the Commission's internal administrative organization and reforms. There was, however, consensus on the need for discussion of structural issues in the IGC to avoid interfering with the internal reorganization and administrative reforms being undertaken by the Commission and its president.

Size of the Commission

As currently constituted, the Commission consists of twenty members including its president. At present it must include at least one national from each member state, but may not include more than two members having the same nationality. There are currently two members from Germany, Spain, France, Italy and the United Kingdom. In general commissioners are usually former ministers or senior civil servants, and in some cases former Prime Ministers like the current Commission President, Romano Prodi. Simply extrapolating the current situation to a Union of 27 member states would result in a Commission of 33 members, with the prospect of further expansion with subsequent accessions.

The starting point for the Conference was the existing treaty provisions, in particular the protocol on the institutions with the prospect of enlargement (see Box 2.1), where the size of the Commission was explicitly singled out as one of the issues to be addressed by the IGC. Moreover, this protocol established a link between the larger member states abandoning the right to nominate a second commissioner and the weighting of votes in the Council (see Chapter 4). The debate was essentially about the optimum number of commissioners in order to maintain an independent, legitimate and efficient Commission after enlargement; however, it inevitably became a debate on the balance of member states' influence. Two radically different approaches were advocated as the best way to marry the principles of independence, legitimacy and effectiveness in a politically strong Commission. Apart from the *status quo* (which was not ruled out by some at the early stages in the negotiation if the overall outcome on Council vote weighting proved inadequate), debate in the Conference became polarized around the following two apparently irreconcilable options:

• The first was a Commission made up of *one national from each member state*. Three main arguments were marshalled in support of this approach. It was considered to be the only way of safeguarding the Commission's legitimacy and acceptability in the eyes of the public by reassuring political opinion in all member states that all relevant sensitivities would be taken into consideration when defining the general interest. An increased number of members was also considered to be compatible with the aim of efficiency in view of the likelihood of increased workload after enlargement. Many advocates of this position also emphasized that it was the only approach which could constitute for them a politically sellable outcome presentable to national parliaments. Moreover, the link established in Article 1 of the Protocol on the institutions (Article 2 notwithstanding) was seen by many, particularly 'smaller' member states, as already having enshrined in the treaty the principle of one commissioner nominated by each member state as a 'done deal' for accepting Council vote re-weighting.

• The second approach was a Commission made up of a *fixed number of commissioners*, whatever the number of member states in the Union. Three compelling arguments were also advanced in favour of this approach. It was considered to be the only way of respecting the spirit and ethos of the treaty by ensuring that the Commission is an independent, supranational body in which commissioners are not representatives of national governments. A Commission limited in size would be easier to manage as a collective unit, thereby enhancing collegiality. It would also help ensure that the Commission could act consistently and effectively, which many felt would not be possible in a college of thirty or more members which would ultimately resemble a debating chamber rather than an executive body.

The Commission itself did not formally plump for one option or the other. It analysed the consequences which would need to be drawn if either one of these approaches were to be adopted by the Conference. It accordingly indicated that the first option would need to be combined with measures fundamentally reorganizing the Commission's internal structure so it could operate effectively with so many members. The latter approach would require cast iron treaty guarantees governing a system of automatic rotation of different nationalities in the Commission placing member states on a strictly equal footing.

The dichotomy between these two approaches illustrates clearly, albeit on a somewhat grander scale than routine Community business, the conflict which often arises in the Union between, on the one hand, intellectually appealing or rational outcomes and, on the other, solutions which are commanded by the political realities and climate in which the Union operates. The second option may be the most rational reflection of the spirit and ethos of an independent Commission in which member states are not 'represented'. Since it is not an inter-governmental body there is no reason why there should be one national from each member state. Indeed, if the argument were pushed to its logical conclusion, one might contend that preference should be given to smaller member states in the composition of the Commission, since in defining the general interest, no one is going to forget the interests of Germany or the UK; could the same be said for the interests of Luxembourg or Slovenia in the absence of a commissioner of these nationalities? However, in many small and medium-sized member states, which view the Commission as their natural ally and defender of their interests, national parliaments had taken a firm line in favour of retaining the right to nominate a national to the Commission. In such circumstances, it would be politically inconceivable for a prime minister to return to his national parliament with the message that not only was that state's voting strength in the Council diminished, but unanimity had been abandoned in some nationally sensitive policy areas, and, moreover, the automatic right to nominate a member of the Commission would immediately be relinquished!

The main handling difficulty was that this became yet another issue impinging on the balance of power between the 'larger' and 'smaller' member states. This posed a particular problem for the incoming French presidency. Since the Amsterdam IGC, France had been one of the most vociferous advocates of a Commission restricted in size. Given that France had publicly heralded a fixed-size Commission as one of its key objectives for the IGC, it was a matter of political credibility for France to achieve a result on this issue. However, the very first ministerial conclave during the French presidency on 24 July only served to further polarize opinion, with the presidency being accused in the press by certain member states of not only producing a biased discussion paper but, worse still, of failing to listen and take account of majority opinion around the table. Moreover, certain member states were quick to highlight the fact that they considered the presidency's rhetoric to be somewhat disingenuous: on the one hand, it claimed to be driven by the desire to maintain a strong and independent Commission in the future; on the other, it was telling that President Chirac, in his speech on the future of Europe to the Bundestag on 27 June, made no mention of the Commission in his institutional blueprint for the future. Some also expressed the view that a fixed-size Commission without a German, French, British, Italian or Spanish commissioner for a particular term of office would be a politically weaker Commission.

Discussion came to a head at the Biarritz informal European Council in October. The hard talking which took place over dinner in Biarritz, which went well beyond the customary independence, legitimacy and efficiency arguments to touch on the very *raison d'être* of the Union and the place and status of its member states, could be interpreted in two ways: either it reflected genuine tension among heads of governments which could imperil the chances of striking a deal in Nice, or it constituted a sign of grim determination on their part to discuss frankly issues relating to the balance among member states in the Union in order to signal what would and what would not be possible in Nice. Biarritz represented a turning point, which altered the terms of the debate in the final run-up to Nice. All five member states abandoning the right to nominate a second commissioner backed the presidency's call for a Commission restricted in size. All of them also accepted the fact that this would require an automatic rotation system among nationals from different member states which placed all member states on the same footing, and were therefore prepared to accept the consequence of this approach: a Commission without a commissioner of their nationality for a term of office. More importantly, perhaps, than the solidarity displayed by the five most populous member states, a number of other member states also accepted the possible need to cap the size of the Commission at a later date, once the Union had grown beyond 25 or 27 members, provided that a strict system of rotation was applied and all member states were treated on an equal footing in terms of nominating nationals for the Commission.

This provided the key to reconciling the two approaches, by opening a window for finding a point of equilibrium based on a so-called 'deferred capping' solution. As early as 24 May, the Portuguese presidency had intimated a possible third option in one of its discussion papers (IGC 2000a) which would have involved fixing a maximum number of commissioners, while retaining one national from each member state until after the first enlargement, and leaving entirely open the question of the definitive size of the Commission after a second enlargement, without prejudging a final decision. This idea was given short shrift by representatives at the time, since many felt that by leaving a final decision to a later date, the problem would remain unresolved. There was consensus on the need to avoid a temporary or partial outcome, which could in any way be construed as a 'Nice leftover'.

Following Biarritz, it became clear that in order to be viable, any solution would need to uphold the principle of one national from each member state in the Commission for the time being. If the principle of a fixed-size Commission was to be accepted in Nice, it could only be contemplated towards the end of the present enlargement process, subject to two absolute conditions: a system of rotation would have to be devised which placed each member state on a strictly equal footing in nominating nationals for the Commission, and that any changes in the internal structure of the Commission, over and above strengthening the position of its president, must preserve the same legal status and voting rights for all commissioners. It was, however, far from certain that all member states would accept such an approach, given the insistence of certain delegations even after Biarritz on a Commission with one national from each member state. The French presidency, in the immediate aftermath of Biarritz, accepted publicly that some form of deferred capping would be sought (*Agence Europe* 2001) rather than braving the face of political implausibility by insisting on a capped Commission from 2005. The key negotiating points which formed the elements of the final agreement were the following:

- The *timing* of any change in the size of the Commission. For practical reasons, it would be easier to envisage a switchover when a new Commission takes up office rather than some other date coinciding with enlargement, with the attendant complication of having to remove sitting commissioners. Since the next Commission will take office in January 2005, Council vote reweighting would apply from the same date, given the linkage laid down in the Amsterdam protocol. It is worth noting that the Treaty of Nice says nothing about the number of commissioners Poland would have up to 1 January 2005 in the event of acceding to the Union prior to that date; this matter will be addressed in its treaty of accession.

- *Deferred capping* of the Commission. Following Biarritz, agreement existed on a Commission for 2005–10 composed of one national from each member state. Two key questions had to be resolved: whether a fixed-size Commission could be envisaged for 2010 and whether the definitive size of the Commission could already be fixed in the Treaty of Nice. In the end, rather than linking a move to a fixed size Commission to the date when a particular Commission would take up office, heads of government decided that it should be linked to the Union reaching a given size: 27 members. This figure now constitutes an absolute maximum (subject to a possible temporary overshoot in the event of subsequent accessions before a new Commission takes office) irrespective of whether or not the 27 member states are those listed in the declaration setting out the common negotiating position of the member states attached to the treaty. As far as the Commission's final size is concerned, the presidency in its initial compromise proposal, endeavoured to fix a maximum of 20 commissioners. However, heads of government finally agreed to amend Article 213(1) to enshrine in the treaty the principle that 'the number of members of the Commission shall be less than the number of Member states', without fixing a definitive number. This will be decided by the Council after the treaty of accession for the 27th member of the Union has been signed (see Article 4 of the protocol on enlargement in Appendix 1.1).
- The treaty provisions governing a *rotation system*. A fixed-size Commission would require cast iron guarantees in the treaty regarding the system of rotation to be put in place. This clearly required more than simply stating that such a rotation system should be based on the principle of equality, or that member states should be treated on a strictly equal footing as regards determination of the sequence of and the time spent by their nationals in the Commission. While this language is written into Article 4 of the protocol, the key provision is the arithmetical formula which reads 'the difference between the total number of terms of office held by nationals of any given pair of

Member states may never be more than one'. This formula was originally contained in the presidency report to the Feira European Council (IGC 2000c), and was retained because it provided an absolute guarantee for all member states. Detailed implementing arrangements for the rotation system will be adopted by the Council after the signature of the treaty of accession of the 27th member state.

- The right of *acceding member states to nominate a national for the Commission*. It was considered important, whatever the final outcome on the Commission, that any acceding member state should have the right to nominate a commissioner until the Commission subsequent to their accession is appointed. This principle has accordingly been enshrined in Article 4 of the protocol, and implies that the 27th acceding state will be able to nominate a commissioner for the remainder of the term of the Commission in office at the time of accession.

The concluding section of this chapter explains why the outcome just described represents a much more ambitious outcome than originally envisaged at the start of the Conference.

Internal Structure and Organization of the Commission

Questions relating to the Commission's size and its internal organization and structure were linked. In the early stages of the negotiations, given the real possibility of ending up with a Commission of one national from each member state, the issue of internal structure was given considerable emphasis. Discussion focused mainly on establishing possible functional hierarchies in the Commission without creating two categories of commissioner with different voting status or rights inside the college which was deemed politically unacceptable. The question was whether the optimum solution was to organize a functional hierarchy 'upwards' through the creation of additional vice-president posts, or 'downwards' by allowing for commissioners without portfolios. Three avenues were explored in the Conference's work, with the final package consisting of a combination of the first two.

Increasing the President's Powers

While treaty provisions are only one of several factors which determine the president's power and influence, such as working practices, convention and the personal qualities and political vision of the incumbent, they nevertheless convey a political signal and provide a basis on which a president can consolidate his or her authority in the Commission. The Treaty of Amsterdam already entrusted the president with the task of exercising political guidance over the work of the Commission (Article 219, first subparagraph, which has now been moved to Article 217(1)—see Box 3.1). A number of elements which already existed in the declaration on the president's powers included in the final act of the Treaty of Amsterdam have been brought into the treaty. Article 217 (see Box 3.1) extends and defines the president's powers, while at the same time enshrining explicitly in the treaty the collegiate nature of the Commission and the principle of collective responsibility. Taken in combination, they balance greater presidential authority with the need for collegiality, although the president will in future enjoy considerable discretionary powers in directing the Commission, conferring a status which is much more than *primus inter pares.*

Box 3.1: Article 217 TEC as amended by the Treaty of Nice

Article 217

1. The Commission shall work under the political guidance of its President, who shall decide on its internal organisation in order to ensure that it acts consistently, efficiently and on the basis of collegiality.
2. The responsibilities incumbent upon the Commission shall be structured and allocated among its Members by its President. The President may reshuffle the allocation of these responsibilities during the Commission's term of office. The Members of the Commission shall carry out the duties devolved upon them by the President under his authority.
3. After obtaining the approval of the College, the President shall appoint Vice-Presidents from among its Members.
4. A member of the Commission shall resign if the President so requests after obtaining the approval of the College.

Strengthening the president's powers proved to be a relatively uncontroversial move, since it was regarded as essential to reinforce the means at the president's disposal for exercising political leadership in the Commission and bolstering collegiality. Many, particularly those advocating a Commission with one national from each member state, also supported strengthened presidential powers for tactical reasons as a means of obviating the need for establishing any new functional hierarchies within the Commission's structure. Others considered that a president with strong powers was essential in order to stamp his or her authority on a Commission which, at least initially, will increase in size. One further highly significant change relating to the president of the Commission was made at Nice. In future he or she will be appointed by the Council at the level of heads of state or government acting by qualified majority. This represents one of the surprises agreed at Nice as part of the final package, given the fact that most member states were reluctant to countenance such a change until that point. It means that in future it will be impossible to have a situation such as in 1994 at Corfu where John Major vetoed the candidacy of Jean-Luc Dehaene as Commission president.

Creating Additional Vice-President Posts
At present the Commission can appoint two vice-presidents. Some delegations supported the creation of up to six or eight vice-presidents to coordinate and oversee the Commission's work in certain areas. This proposal, originally made by the UK, was regarded with certain suspicion at the outset since it was viewed by some as potentially establishing a 'directorate' run by the larger member states inside the Commission. The question was: if the number of vice-president posts were to be increased, how many should there be? At the end of the day, the treaty did not set a figure, leaving the number to be appointed during the term of office of the Commission at the president's discretion. Vice-presidents will in future be appointed by the president rather than by the Commission, although the college will have to give its prior approval.

Creating Commissioners without Portfolio
The rationale behind this suggestion was to structure the Commission's tasks into around 15–20 portfolios corresponding to the Commission's core responsibilities and to allocate coordinating or other specific tasks to commissioners without a portfolio. This could be achieved in different ways, such as by writing a maximum number of portfolios into the treaty without specifying their content. However, many delegations considered that such an approach would result *de facto* in two categories of commissioner: one supported by administrative structures, and the other without. Differentiating between commissioners in this way, albeit in purely functional terms, led to calls for guarantees to ensure a balance between nationals from different member states over time, thus replicating the same types of problem of ensuring balance between the

member states in a Commission with fewer members than member states. Article 217 in the Treaty of Nice makes no specific mention of the way in which the Commission will be structured; this has been left entirely at the discretion of the president, although it would probably be politically difficult to envisage a future president creating commissioners without portfolio. Given that the principle of a fixed-size Commission has been enshrined in the treaty, it became less important to pursue this issue in Nice.

Accountability Issues

Considerable emphasis is placed on the link between the Commission's independence and its political accountability. Calls were made for the IGC to explore in greater detail two types of accountability issue. The first was whether steps should be taken to reinforce the *collective* accountability of the college in the Union's institutional setup; the second related to the need to enhance the political responsibility of *individual* commissioners, particularly in the light of events which led to the downfall of the Santer Commission on 15 March 1999.

Collective Accountability
The Commission is formally accountable to the European Parliament by virtue of the fact that the Commission as a body may be subject to a vote of censure. The European Parliament must also approve the nominee for the post of president of the Commission and must subsequently approve the president and the members of the Commission as a body before they can be formally appointed by the Council. The notion of political responsibility of the Commission is closely tied up with the need for it to preserve its independence vis-à-vis member states, other Union institutions and private interests. Over the years, criticism has been voiced at the fact that the Commission has perhaps drifted closer to the European Parliament than perhaps desirable given its special institutional role. Some member states accordingly deemed a measure of 'repositioning' the Commission apex of the institutional triangle necessary, in particular by clarifying in the treaty the nature of its political responsibility in order to counteract a tendency for accountability to be construed as detailed supervision of the Commission's activities. This trend might not only risk compromising its independence but is also at odds with the very principle of political accountability which

should allow an executive body the leeway necessary to be judged on its implementation of a political programme without its activities being micro-managed.

The Conference examined two ideas designed to redress this perceived weakness in the institutional system. The first was to allow the president of the Commission, with the support of the college, to seek the confidence of the European Parliament as a means of strengthening the Commission's political position vis-à-vis the Parliament. The presidency's report to the Feira European Council included a draft treaty provision to this effect (IGC 2000c). Some delegations felt, however, that the ability to seek a vote of confidence from the Parliament immediately raised the question of whether it should go hand in hand with a right for the Commission to dissolve the Parliament. This, however, raised fundamental questions that went well beyond the Conference's remit. The second was a proposal to enhance the Commission's political accountability to the Council or the European Council possibly by seeking a vote of confidence. Given the generally acknowledged objective of the Conference not to alter substantially the institutional balance, it was considered premature to pursue these issues further at this stage. It is likely, however, that issues of this type will resurface in the debate leading up to and during the next IGC in 2004.

Individual Accountability of Commissioners
The political responsibility of individual commissioners was propelled to the forefront of the political agenda when the entire Santer Commission tendered their resignations in March 1999. Strong fears were voiced, however, that holding individual commissioners politically to account (whether to the European Parliament or the European Council) might both seriously undermine the principle of collegiality and constitute a radical and undesirable shift in the institutional balance by exposing individual commissioners to pressures that could impair their independence. The commitment to resign if asked, which President Prodi obtained from each prospective member of the college when constituting his new Commission, was widely supported, although views were initially divided about whether this informal arrangement (the so-called *lex Prodi*) should be codified in the treaty. The Commission and a significant number of delegations, however, considered that it would be useful to include expressly in the treaty the obligation incumbent on a member of the Commission to resign if the president requests him or

her to do so, subject to seeking the collective approval of the Commission before issuing such a request (see Box 3.1). Holding individual commissioners politically to account to the president presents the least risk of undermining the collegiality of the Commission. President Prodi has already agreed to take it extremely seriously if the European Parliament passes a resolution of 'no confidence' in a commissioner. It would not have formal effect, but it would be a serious political signal that Prodi would ignore at his peril (Jacobs 2000).

Other Issues

Apart from the above points, the voluntary resignation of the entire college in March 1999 gave rise to discussion about the need to clarify the treaty provisions on the resignation of members of the Commission and their obligations after leaving office. There was general agreement, however, that the current treaty provisions had enabled the crisis to be weathered without any insurmountable problems, that an event of this type was quite exceptional and that it would be difficult to lay down treaty provisions to cope with every possible eventuality. In considering these questions, the Conference decided that a number of tidying up amendments should be made to Article 215 (see Box 3.2).

Box 3.2: Article 215 TEC as amended by the Treaty of Nice

Article 215

Apart from normal replacement, or death, the duties of a Member of the Commission shall end when he resigns or is compulsorily retired.

A vacancy caused by resignation, compulsory retirement or death shall be filled for the remainder of the Member's term of office by a new Member appointed by the Council acting by qualified majority. The Council may, acting unanimously, decide that such a vacancy need not be filled.

In the event of resignation, compulsory retirement or death, the President shall be replaced for the remainder of his term of office. The procedure laid down in Article 214(2) shall be applicable for the replacement of the President.

Save in the case of compulsory retirement under Article 216, Members of the Commission shall remain in office until they have been replaced or until the Council has decided not to fill a vacancy as provided for in the second paragraph of this article.

A Manageable and Effective College for the Future

The issue of the size of the Commission had to be resolved at Nice. The fact that the Conference agreed to cap the Commission, albeit at a later date, was a far more ambitious outcome than could have been envisaged even half way through the negotiation. Before the IGC began, this outcome was discounted as a 'non-starter' (Petite 2000). Any watering down of the final text, for example by simply allowing the possibility for the Council to decide to limit the number of commissioners in future, would inevitably have been regarded as creating a 'Nice leftover' and heads of government would have been sharply rebuked for shirking the issue. Moreover, the chances of a decision actually being taken at a later date to cap the Commission once the principle of one commissioner of each nationality had been accepted at Nice would have been slim, to say the least.

The final outcome has nevertheless been criticized because the treaty failed to fix a definitive size for the Commission. Even respectable commentators have perhaps been a little over-hasty in their initial assessments. Some have misread the outcome as failure to decide anything on the size of the Commission (Riccardi 2001). The fact that the Treaty of Nice does not stipulate a final size for the Commission is relatively unimportant. The crucial point was to decide on a fixed-size Commission and the key principles governing the system of rotation. The lack of a maximum number of commissioners is in fact an optical illusion deployed to enable acceptance of the final outcome. A viable and politically credible system of rotation will require a substantial gap between the maximum number of commissioners and the number of member states. It would be politically untenable to have, for example a Union of 27 member states with a Commission of 26 or 25 members. Which member states would be forced to draw the short straw in nominations for the first capped Commission? In practice, any politically realistic system is likely to involve a maximum number of commissioners not too far removed from that initially proposed by the presidency (20). This will occur from the date on which the Commission takes up its duties following the accession of the 27th member state. The only open question is whether this will occur prior to the Commission which takes up office in 2010 or 2015.

This result was achieved because the French presidency deployed a strategy, albeit somewhat heavy-handedly at times, with a clear objective and steered the negotiation towards that objective. Having a strategy paid off. In the meantime, the Commission will become larger; this was the political price to pay for a capped Commission. However, judicious use by the Commission president of his or her powers and the organizational means afforded to him or her under the treaty should ensure a manageable and effective college in the intervening period and beyond.

4 |

The Weighting of Votes in the Council

Vote weighting refers to the voting strength given to each of the Council's members (i.e. national government representatives) when decisions are taken by qualified majority. Since qualified majority voting is now used for most Council decision-making, voting clout is an issue. Under the current system in EU-15 prior to Nice, the four largest members each have ten votes, while the smallest, Luxembourg, has two votes (see Table 4.1). The need for a change in the system prior to enlargement had already been accepted in principle at Amsterdam. The IGC had to decide how this should be done.

At Nice, this is the issue that detained heads of government the longest and was the last to be settled at around 4.20 am on the Monday morning at the end of the longest summit in the Union's history. This question more than any other was all too readily seized on by the media as a 'big' *versus* 'small' power struggle. It is easy to understand why; after all, the Council of the European Union is designed as the institutional vehicle for articulating the interests of member state governments in the Union's legislative and executive decision-making processes. A shift in the relative voting strength of any individual member is easy to portray as a measurable change in the relative power and influence of that member state in determining negotiating outcomes. Hence, it appeared easier on this issue to single out 'winners' and 'losers' than on some of the other more arcane institutional reform questions.

Appearances, however, can be deceptive. As far as member states' voting strength is concerned, a distinction has to be drawn between voting *weight* and voting *power*, both of which are important. Voting weight refers to the relative voting strength accorded to any individual member state under a system of weighted votes, that is, the percentage of the total vote held by each member of the Council. Voting power refers to the ability of any individual member of the Council to cast a decisive vote for adopting or blocking a decision, that is, the likelihood of a member of the Council being instrumental in constructing a winning or blocking coalition. This depends not only on the actual number of votes held, but also on the threshold for achieving a qualified majority or a 'blocking minority' as well as on the likelihood of other like-minded members of the Council joining a coalition. The difference between the two concepts can be graphically illustrated by considering the original system of weighting in the Union of six. France, Germany and Italy each had four votes, the Netherlands and Belgium each had two and Luxembourg had one. A qualified majority required twelve votes out of seventeen in favour. While Luxembourg's voting *weight* was one out of seventeen (or 5.9% of total votes), its voting *power* was zero, since its single vote was never required to form any qualified majority of twelve votes, nor any blocking minority of six votes! The design of this system is explained in greater detail below.

Table 4.1: Weightings and population for EU-15

Members of the Council	Votes	Population (000s)
Germany	10	82165
United Kingdom	10	59623
France	10	58747
Italy	10	57680
Spain	8	39442
Netherlands	5	15864
Greece	5	10546
Belgium	5	10239
Portugal	5	9998
Sweden	4	8861
Austria	4	8092
Denmark	3	5330
Finland	3	5171
Ireland	3	3775
Luxembourg	2	436
Total EU	87	375969

Total votes = 87	Votes	% Votes	Minimum number of members	Minimum % of population
Qualified majority	62	71.26	8	58.16
Blocking minority	26	29.89	3	12.38

Eurostat population data 2000.

An extensive body of academic literature exists attempting to measure voting power of members of the Council on the basis of various power-value indices, such as the Shapley-Shubik or the Banzhaf indices (Hosli 1996; Winkler 1998). An interesting independent quantitative analysis of the various voting systems on the table for Nice was carried out comparing their relative merits in terms of efficiency, legitimacy and acceptability (Baldwin *et al.* 2000).

While such indices and quantitative analyses may provide revealing insights into the power of an individual member of the Council to shape decisions or into the statistical likelihood of successful decision-making outcomes, they do not in themselves provide a failsafe guide for selecting a new system of vote weighting which is largely determined by political factors difficult to quantify. Altering the system required calculations by individual governments of more than the way in which the overall legitimacy and efficiency of the system would be affected, important though these are. The primary concern was the way in which national voting strength and power would be affected. Other factors included broader political linkages to other issues, in particular the distribution of seats in the European Parliament and the need to 'compensate' member states for foregoing the right to nominate a second commissioner. Also, probably the most important factor was the perceived political 'saleability' of any outcome to national parliaments and the general public. This issue, perhaps more than any other, was as much about public presentation of the outcome as about the substance and impact of the changes agreed.

The politics of presentation lent a further layer of complexity to the process of negotiation. Because of this fact, much of the work in the early stages of the Conference concentrated on examining the features of various systems of Council vote weighting, including alternative approaches suggested by certain delegations, as well as the various political parameters which would need to be borne in mind in reaching an acceptable outcome. The presidency only put forward an actual proposal containing figures at Nice itself. However, the preliminary groundwork was essential to ensure that everyone was converging towards a point of equilibrium as a final compromise, and that the technical ramifications of different models had been grasped, with heads of government left to decide the eminently political question of 'how much'.

Portraying the issue as a confrontation pitting large against small ignores three facts about Union decision-making. The first is the extent to which the current institutional arrangements have been devised and evolved since their inception precisely to ease large versus small state concerns. The second is that within the Council, a regular large/small split practically never occurs in reality. Alliances form and disband on the basis of shared or discrete negotiating objectives which are determined by national interests and priorities rather than size (Hayes-Renshaw and Wallace 1997). The third is the way in which qualified majority voting lends a dynamic to negotiating in the Council in which member states are forced to seek compromises, to consider what their key bottom-line objectives are and to focus their negotiating effort accordingly. This dynamic goes some way towards explaining why the Council is often more than simply the sum of its fifteen component members seeking least-common-denominator solutions and possesses its own supranational institutional 'culture'. The Council, supported by its preparatory bodies, has developed into a well-oiled machine in which the interests of governments with very different national priorities and political complexions can be reconciled in outcomes (often with the help of the Commission) in the interest of the Union as a whole, which, more often than not, represent much more than a minimalist solution. Despite this, palpable tension emerged during the endgame negotiations between less populous member states, which considered that their position was being eroded too far in the Union, and the larger member states, which were seeking to preserve as far as possible their voting clout after enlargement.

The Principle of Weighted Votes in the Existing System

That members of the Council of different sizes should be given different voting weights is not as self-evident as might be assumed. The basic principle underlying all organizations or groupings of states in international law is the sovereign equality of states; in other words 'one state, one vote'. This is the case when the Council is deciding by unanimity (for quasi-constitutional or politically sensitive matters) or by simple majority (in a limited number of mainly procedural matters). In fact, simple majority is the default voting rule in the treaty unless it provides otherwise, which it usually does.

Box 4.1: Description of the pre-Nice system of Council vote weighting

The pre-Nice weighting system for EU-15 ranges from ten votes each to the four largest member states to two votes for Luxembourg (see Table 4.1). Relative population size is not reflected in an absolute, linear way, but is based on a political agreement reflecting the principle of 'degressive proportionality'. In other words, the less populous member states are over-represented in terms of voting strength (i.e. their percentage of total votes is greater than their percentage of the EU population), while larger member states are under-represented (i.e. their percentage of total votes is lower than their percentage of the EU population). This represents a compromise between the principle of 'one state, one vote' and 'one citizen, one vote', reflecting the dual nature of the Union as a Union of both peoples and of states.

The system was constructed so as to ensure a certain relationship between member states based on a system of 'groups' or 'clusters' of large, medium and small member states, with states in each cluster having an identical number of votes. In 1957, the threshold for determining a qualified majority was fixed to ensure that the three large states (France, Germany and Italy) voting together could achieve a majority and could not be prevented form moving forward against the combined opposition of the Benelux. However, the opposition of any one of the large member states, even with Luxembourg, would not be sufficient to block a decision. Prior to the Treaty of Nice, the system had the following characteristics:

- Apart from an adjustment in voting weights to accommodate new categories of member states at the first enlargement in 1973, the system has undergone straightforward extrapolation at each successive enlargement.
- The system of 'clusters' was maintained. With each successive enlargement, new member states were categorized in accordance with the same principle, although additional categories had to be inserted into the system as required on the basis of member states' size (e.g. Denmark and Ireland were allocated three votes each, Spain eight votes and Austria and Sweden four votes each).
- The threshold for achieving a qualified majority in terms of weighted votes remained practically unchanged for each successive configuration of the EU at around 71% of total votes (currently 62 out of 87 votes, or 71.26%).
- The minimum population of the Union represented by qualified majority (i.e. forming a qualified majority with members with the highest voting strength compared to their population—that is, starting with the least populous member State and counting up until a qualified majority is achieved) was 67.81% in 1957 (EU-6), but, following an initial blip after the first enlargement to 70.49% (EU-9), steadily declined following successive enlargements to 70.13% (EU-10), 63.21% (EU-12) to 58.16% (EU-15) in 2000.

- A qualified majority always represented at least half of the member states as an automatic, in-built feature (i.e. not as a separate necessary criterion). The treaty has, however, always provided for a specific threshold in terms of numbers of member states when the Council is deciding on a basis other than a Commission proposal (two thirds of the member states).

Outside the European Union, examples of formally unequal representation of states at international level tends to be the exception rather than the rule—for example, in the United Nations Security Council where the permanent members (the United States, France, the United Kingdom, Russia and China) effectively have the right to veto, and in international financial institutions where voting power is directly linked to capital share. Unequal weighting can also be found in systems of representation within states. One example is of the German Confederation between 1815 and 1866, where, in the Plenary Assembly, votes were distributed among the 41 states and a voting threshold was set at two-thirds of the votes. This ensured that Austria and Prussia, the largest states representing some 58% of the population, even if they acted together with the four kingdoms of Bavaria, Saxony, Hanover and Wurtemburg, could not outvote the rest (Best 2000). Modern day examples also exist in federal or confederal states such as Germany and Switzerland where the upper parliamentary chamber provides for differentiated voting strength of the component entities on the basis of size. However, the Council of the European Union, given its powers and composition, cannot be compared to an upper parliamentary chamber.

The main purpose of a system of weighted votes in the Council today, as in the German Confederation in the early nineteenth century, is to ensure a reasonable 'balance of influence' between member states of different sizes when decisions are being taken. The present system was constructed during the negotiations that gave birth to the Treaty of Rome in 1957. The principle of applying a weighting to the votes of the member states was itself fairly readily accepted: a system of weighting had applied in the ECSC Treaty. However, it was felt that a new system was required to reflect the new reality of a common market, and the question was how to determine the relative size of the votes to be attributed to each member state (De l'Ecotais 1996a, 1996b, 1997).

While several 'objective' criteria could be envisaged for determining the relative 'weight' of each member state, it was clear at an early stage that a purely arithmetical and linear extrapolation of any objective criteria would lead to unacceptable political results. Three criteria were considered: population size, economic weight (national income or GNP) and budget contributions. The first two would give incredibly high and politically unrealistic values for the large member states. Using budget contributions as a criterion was also problematic because although the Community was to be funded by national contributions for a transitional period, the treaty foresaw the possibility of moving to a system of 'own resources' (which indeed happened in 1970). In establishing a permanent weighting system, a clever political balance was struck in 1957 in the relative weightings accorded to each member state and in the ability of the member states to construct winning or blocking coalitions.

The solution was to distinguish between three groups of states—large member states (Germany, France and Italy) which would each have four votes, medium-sized member states (the Netherlands and Belgium), which would each have two votes, and small member states (Luxembourg), which would have one vote. This gave a total of seventeen votes. The critical political question, and one that has remained a real political bone of contention ever since in determining voting power (including at Nice), was where to fix the threshold in terms of votes for a qualified majority. Fixing the threshold at twelve votes out of seventeen for EU-6 meant that:

- the qualified majority represented 70.6% of the votes in the Council;
- the minimum population represented by a qualified majority was 67.8%;
- at least half the number of member states would be required to constitute a qualified majority—the three most populous ($3 \times 4 = 12$);
- the three medium-sized and small member states themselves could not block a decision ($2 + 2 + 1 = 5$). In other words, they had insufficient votes to constitute what in Union jargon is referred to as a 'blocking minority';
- two-thirds of the member states were required to vote in favour when measures were decided on a basis other than a Commission proposal. Although this provision did not have many practical applications, it gave Luxembourg voting power in circumstances where the safeguard of a Commission proposal did not exist. This provision comes into play much more frequently now under the second and third pillars.

It should be remembered that at the outset of the Community, unanimity was the general rule for voting in the Council, and qualified majority voting very much the exception. It was only after the entry into force of the Single European Act in 1987 that the issue of Council vote weighting again came to the fore with the significant extension of qualified majority voting associated with the creation of the single market. Vote weighting has become such a key political issue because qualified majority voting now applies for most decisions taken in the Council (see Chapter 5).

Following successive enlargements (to nine in 1973 with the accession of Denmark, Ireland and the UK, ten in 1981 with the accession of Greece, twelve in 1986 with the accession of Spain and Portugal, and fifteen in 1995 with the entry of Austria, Finland and Sweden), the system was adjusted without changing its fundamental character. Table 4.2 shows that the threshold for the qualified majority in terms of votes remained more or less constant at around 71%.

Table 4.2: Evolution of the QMV threshold in terms of votes

EU-6	EU-9	EU-10	EU-12	EU-15
70.59%	70.69%	71.43%	71.05%	71.26%

The Limits of the Pre-Nice Weighting System

If the current voting system had served the Union reasonably well, why could the Conference not just simply agree to continue extrapolating it as the Union enlarged as it had done on previous occasions? There were essentially three reasons why the system had to be changed.

The first was the formal requirement enshrined in the treaty to 'compensate' the larger member states for relinquishing the right to nominate a second commissioner through the system of Council vote weighting. While this linkage always tacitly existed during the Amsterdam IGC, the protocol on the institutions with the prospect of enlargement annexed to the treaties (see Chapter 2) explicitly mentioned this requirement as one of the relevant factors to be taken into account in the new system of weighting.

The second was the impact on the voting strength of the most populous states of admitting a large number of small and medium-sized candidate states. Some argued that the impact of successive enlargements had been borne *equally* by all member states, large and small. This is certainly true if one considers the relative reduction in each *individual* member state's percentage share of the total vote. In other words, following the accession of Sweden, Austria and Finland, Germany's share of the total votes fell from 10/76 to 10/87. Luxembourg's share fell from 2/76 to 2/87. In both cases this represents a loss of just over 12.5% in voting strength (i.e. the percentage of total votes added through the new accessions). However, the view that all members of the Council were equally affected by enlargements was challenged by the more populous member states, which argued that a relative loss of voting power penalized to a greater extent states whose population sizes under the system was already 'under-represented' in terms of voting strength than smaller member states who were already 'over-represented' in terms of their population size. This warranted, in their eyes, an increase in the number of votes for the largest member states.

Third, a potential political legitimacy problem was in the making. Over successive enlargements the minimum percentage of the Union's population represented by a qualified majority had steadily declined from 67% to 58% in 2000. If the current system were simply extrapolated to EU-27, the minimum population threshold for a qualified majority would decline to 50.2% (see Table 4.3). The explanation for this decline lies in the *degressive proportionality* of the system. Since successive accessions in future will involve a high proportion of small and medium-sized states, a larger share of the total votes will be held by countries that have a proportionately higher share of votes compared to their population size. Given the substantial increase in qualified majority voting that has occurred since the Single Act in 1987, the legitimacy argument has come increasingly to the forefront of debate, even if some member states saw no problem in coming down to a minimum of just over 50%. If the Conference wished to halt or reverse this trend under the current system, this could only be achieved by giving the larger member states more votes—that is, ensuring a greater correlation between voting strength and population without necessarily calling into question the principle of degressive proportionality.

Table 4.3: Linear extrapolation of the EU-15 weighting system to EU-27

Members of the Council	Votes	Population (000s)
Germany	10	82165
United Kingdom	10	59623
France	10	58747
Italy	10	57680
Spain	8	39442
Poland	8	38654
Romania	6	22456
Netherlands	5	15864
Greece	5	10546
Czech Republic	5	10278
Belgium	5	10239
Hungary	5	10043
Portugal	5	9998
Sweden	4	8861
Bulgaria	4	8191
Austria	4	8092
Slovakia	3	5399
Denmark	3	5330
Finland	3	5171
Ireland	3	3775
Lithuania	3	3699
Latvia	3	2424
Slovenia	3	1988
Estonia	3	1439
Cyprus	2	755
Luxembourg	2	436
Malta	2	380
Total EU-27	134	481675

Total votes = 134	Votes	% Votes	Minimum number of members	Minimum % of population
Qualified majority	96	71.64	14	50.20
Blocking minority	39	29.10	4	10.50

Eurostat population data 2000.

A New System of Vote Weighting: Revolution or Evolution?

The IGC negotiators were not starting with a blank sheet of paper. As a so-called Amsterdam 'leftover', the treaty itself, in the Protocol on the institutions, called for the system of vote weighting to be altered either by 'reweighting of the votes or by dual majority, in a manner acceptable to all Member States, taking into account all relevant elements, notably compensating those Member States which give up the possibility of nominating a second member of the Commission'. The Helsinki European Council conclusions also explicitly referred to both reweighting and dual majority systems, as well as the threshold for qualified-majority decision-making as subjects to be examined by the Conference. On this latter point, declaration No. 50 attached to the final act of Amsterdam also stated that the Ioannina compromise (see Box 4.2) would be extended until the entry into force of the first enlargement and that by then, a solution for the special case of Spain would be found.

Different Systems of Council Vote Weighting

As with other key issues, the Conference had to grapple with two problems: addressing the substantive issues and managing a highly politically charged negotiation which, because of its presentational angle, required particularly deft handling.

Initial negotiations during the Portuguese presidency showed that a broad measure of agreement existed on certain principles and features which should underlie the system of Council vote weighting, namely:

- Any system had to reflect the dual nature of the Union as both a Union of states and a Union of peoples.
- The system had to be equitable, transparent, efficient and easily understood by citizens.
- The very legitimacy of the system dictated that any qualified majority had to respect a minimum threshold in terms of population greater than 50%, although opinions ranged widely on what that specific figure should be.
- In addition to the acknowledged link to the size of the Commission, a link was also made to the allocation of seats in the European Parliament (see Chapter 6), particularly given the Parliament's ever increasing co-legislative role with the Council.
- Any system should not make it more difficult for decisions to be taken within the Council.

Box 4.2: The 'Ioannina compromise'

During negotiations leading up to the accession of Austria, Sweden and Finland, the level at which the QMV threshold should be set became a hotly disputed bone of contention. Until 1995, 23 votes (out of 76) were required in the Council for a blocking minority (i.e. two large member states, plus any other member state apart from Luxembourg). If the QMV threshold were to remain at around 71% of votes after enlargement, the number of votes in the blocking minority in absolute terms would increase from 23 to 26. The UK (in order to check the pace of integration) and Spain (ostensibly to protect Mediterranean interests, but more probably linked to Spain's desire to secure similar status in voting terms as other large member states) objected to increasing the blocking threshold in absolute terms, since this would reduce opportunities for constructing blocking alliances in the Council. The member states finally agreed to retain the QMV threshold in terms of votes at the same percentage level after enlargement, thereby increasing the blocking minority to 26 votes, while at the same time adopting the so-called 'Ioannina compromise' agreed by Council decision of 24 March 1994, and framed as follows:

'If members of the Council representing a total of 23 to 25 votes indicate their intention to oppose the adoption by the Council of a decision by qualified majority, the Council will do all in its power to reach, within a reasonable time and without prejudicing the obligatory time limits laid down by the Treaties and by secondary law, such as in Articles 189b and 189c of the Treaty establishing the European Community, a satisfactory solution that can be adopted by at least 65 votes. During this period, and always respecting the Rules of Procedure of the Council, the President undertakes, with the assistance of the Commission, any initiative necessary to facilitate a wider basis of agreement in the Council. The members of the Council lend him their assistance.'

The then UK Prime Minister, John Major, highlighted the character of the decision as a legally binding act. Other member states considered that the content of the decision by the twelve was more political in nature. The impact of the decision depends on the interpretation given to the phrase 'within a reasonable time'. Article 7 of the Council's rules of procedure allow for any member of the Council or the Commission to call for a vote in the Council, and a simple majority could determine whether 'a reasonable time' had elapsed. Contrary to widespread fears at the time, the compromise had little practical effect on decision-making and has to date only been threatened or formally invoked (unsuccessfully) before a ministerial vote on rare occasions (e.g. on 24/25 October 1995, when the UK Agriculture Council was deciding on national compensation for loss of farm income through currency movements).

At Amsterdam, declaration No. 50 attached to the final Act of the Conference relating to the Protocol on the institutions explicitly reaffirmed that 'the "Ioannina compromise" would be extended until the entry into force of the first enlargement and that, by that date, a satisfactory solution would be found for the special case of Spain'. A satisfactory solution has now been found in the Treaty of Nice.

As during the Amsterdam IGC, the various proposals examined by the Conference could be categorized in three general approaches for adjusting the weighting of votes in the Council: a 'simple' dual majority system; a 'weighted' dual majority system; and a 'reweighting' of votes under the existing system. These approaches, and a number of sub-variants, are now analysed to identify the main merits and drawbacks of each.

A 'Simple' Dual Majority System

The 'simple' dual majority system, which was advocated strongly by the Commission and a significant number of delegations right up to the final stages of the Conference, involves setting a dual threshold expressed as:

1. a simple majority of members of the Council;
2. a simple majority of the population of the Union.

The adoption of any measure would be subject to simultaneous compliance with *both* conditions.

The system had obvious advantages: it was entirely objective, reflected clearly the dual nature of the Union, was easy to understand and had the potential to make decision-making easier if it involved lowering the threshold. It was supported for these reasons by the Commission and a number of delegations. However, it also contained a number of flaws which rendered it politically untenable as a compromise formula, despite the fact that this system and some of its variants enjoyed a significant level of support.

First, the system juxtaposed two voting scales (population and number of member states) rather than building both into the voting system as had been the case until then. This created political presentation problems. A system which, on the one hand, would give Germany over 40% more votes than France (under the population weighting) or more than double the votes accorded to Spain, and on the other, would give France or Spain the same number of votes as Luxembourg (under the requirement for a minimum number of Council members to support a decision) would be difficult to defend.

Second, because of this dual threshold, some of the larger member states also considered it did not adequately address the 'compensation' requirement, since any advantage conferred via the population requirement would be negated by the member state criterion.

Third, it would represent a radical departure from a system with a voting power structure built on clusters of member states with similar voting strength.

Fourth, fixing a qualified majority at just over 50% of the Union's population would mean that in a Union of 27 member states, the three largest member states (including Germany) plus Spain, would be unable to muster a blocking minority in the Council.

Fifth, in configurations of the Union with even numbers of member states, the minimum population represented by a blocking minority would fall close to 9%, which many considered would be difficult to defend on legitimacy grounds.

One technical problem encountered at the start of the Nice IGC was precisely how to determine the population element in either of the dual majority options. The Portuguese presidency, in a note submitted to the Preparatory Group on 24 May (IGC 2000b), illustrated a simple and practical way of doing this by constructing a vote weighting table in which each member's voting weight is directly proportional to that member state's share of the total population of the Union, rounded to the nearest tenth of a percentage point and multiplied by ten. This resulted in the weighting table set out in Table 4.4 for EU-27. The advantage of this presentation is that it illustrates immediately the percentage of the Union's population represented by any vote. A qualified majority would require 50.1% of the population in favour (i.e. 501 votes) along with a simple head count to verify that the second condition was met. Having resolved this practical difficulty, the only drawback would be the need to change each member's weighting following each enlargement and to update the weightings in line with population movements.

The 'Weighted' Dual Majority

This option, originally put forward during the Amsterdam IGC, involved retaining a system of weighted votes extrapolated to EU-27, and setting a dual threshold expressed as:

1. a majority in terms of weighted votes (either unchanged or with a slight reweighting);
2. a majority of the total population of the Union (which would logically be set at a figure higher than the percentage resulting from a majority of weighted votes).

The adoption of a measure would require *both* conditions to be met.

Table 4.4: Weighting table for the 'simple' dual majority in EU-27

Members of the Council	Weighting
Germany	170
United Kingdom	123
France	122
Italy	120
Spain	82
Poland	80
Romania	47
Netherlands	33
Greece	22
Czech Republic	21
Belgium	21
Hungary	21
Portugal	21
Sweden	18
Bulgaria	17
Austria	17
Slovakia	11
Denmark	11
Finland	11
Ireland	8
Lithuania	8
Latvia	5
Slovenia	4
Estonia	3
Cyprus	2
Luxembourg	1
Malta	1
Total EU-27	1000

For their adoption, acts of the Council would require at least *501 votes* in favour, cast by at least *a majority of members*.

	Minimum number of members		Weighting	Minimum % of population
Qualified majority	14	*and*	501	50.10
Blocking minority	14	*or*	500	11.62

Table 4.5: Weighting table for a 'weighted' dual majority in EU-27

Members of the Council	Weighting A	Weighting B
Germany	10	170
United Kingdom	10	123
France	10	122
Italy	10	120
Spain	8	82
Poland	8	80
Romania	6	47
Netherlands	5	33
Greece	5	22
Czech Republic	5	21
Belgium	5	21
Hungary	5	21
Portugal	5	21
Sweden	4	18
Bulgaria	4	17
Austria	4	17
Slovakia	3	11
Denmark	3	11
Finland	3	11
Ireland	3	8
Lithuania	3	8
Latvia	3	5
Slovenia	3	4
Estonia	3	3
Cyprus	2	2
Luxembourg	2	1
Malta	2	1
Total EU-27	134	1000

For their adoption, acts of the Council would require at least *96 votes* under weighting A and *580 votes* under weighting B.

	Weighting A		Weighting B	% votes Weighting A	Minimum number of members	Minimum % of population
Qualified majority	96	*and*	580	71.64	14	58.00
Blocking minority	39	*or*	421	29.10	4	10.50

The attraction of this system lay in the fact that it need not necessarily involve the painful process of adjusting the existing weighting of votes, since any reweighting element could be 'concealed' in the population safety net. The proposal was also made to undertake a moderate reweighting of weighting A as a means of helping to address the compensation question. However, measuring the population element of the system would have required laying down in the treaty a *second* weighting table alongside the existing one. For this reason, the proposal was criticized on the same grounds as outlined above for the 'simple' dual majority system, in addition to which there was the mind-numbing complexity of having to work with two new weighted thresholds. Despite the obvious drawbacks of such a model, rendering decision-making in the Council both more complex and more difficult, the outcome in Nice, although ostensibly a reweighting model, bore more than a passing resemblance to the system just described (see below).

'Reweighting' of Votes

The third approach before the Conference involved retaining the system in its existing form and reweighting (i.e. increasing) the votes of the larger member states. As previously mentioned, the Council's present voting system does not reflect the relative size of each member state's population in absolute, linear terms, as under the dual majority approaches described above, but applies a degressively proportional formula resulting from a political approach described earlier in this chapter.

Two strong arguments were marshalled in favour of reweighting: first, that it was the simplest and most effective means of compensating those member states relinquishing the right to nominate a second commissioner; and second, that it could halt the downward trend in the minimum threshold of the EU population represented by a qualified majority as an in-built feature, rather than as a supplementary condition to fulfil. It is axiomatic that the only way to achieve both requirements under the current system would be to give more votes to the larger member states. For these reasons, it was favoured from the outset by most of the larger member states (except Germany which, for obvious reasons, had a preference for dual majority options), although a number of medium-sized states also indicated early on that they were not opposed in principle to reweighting, provided that the operation was limited in scope and did not call into question the overall balance of the system.

The French presidency, while it did not definitively close the door on the dual majority option until Nice, nevertheless considered that, for political reasons, it was unlikely to receive unanimous support, and accordingly concentrated on a reweighting approach as the most likely to secure agreement. Reweighting could at one and the same time safeguard legitimacy in terms of the minimum population represented by a qualified majority, compensate the larger member states for the abandonment of their second commissioner and preserve the clusters of member states with the same voting weights. This latter point was a key issue for France, since France and Germany had parity of voting weight despite the fact that Germany had a population of over 22 million more than France.

Assessment of the Three Systems

None of the vote weighting systems described above is ideal. Table 4.6 compares each of the proposed solutions against ten political para-meters relating to the system of Council vote weighting mentioned during the early stages of the Conference. While this is not a rigorous methodological categorization, it would appear to show that a simple reweighting could in theory address most of the political parameters without radically altering the existing system. However, these indica-tors only provide a rough-and-ready means of comparing the different systems. Within each system adjustments could be made in such a way as to make decision-making more or less difficult. A split soon devel-oped between advocates of a straightforward reweighting of votes, and those who favoured a dual-majority solution, in particular the simple dual majority. For the reasons outlined above, the French presidency preferred to concentrate on simple reweighting options, although the final outcome proved to be somewhat more complicated. The presi-dency's opening bid in Nice was to put on the table a voting range which extended from 3 to 30.

The Nice Solution on Vote Weighting

Six political parameters were crucial in determining the outcome of the Conference:

1. whether reweighting should only apply to those member states giving up the right to nominate a second commissioner;
2. the size of the reweighting;

Table 4.6: Comparative assessment of the three main weighting models

Political criteria	Simple reweighting	'Simple' dual majority	'Weighted' dual majority[a]
Minimum of 58% of the EU population represented by a qualified majority	Yes	No (but possible)	Yes
Clearly identifiable compensation for member states relinquishing the right to nominate a second Commissioner	Yes	No	No
Increased ability for the most populous member states to form qualified majorities *and* blocking minorities	Yes	No	No
Ability for three large member states to block a decision	Yes/No	No	No
Decision-making not rendered more difficult	Yes	Yes	No
Presence of half of the member states in any qualified majority	Yes/No (depending on the size of the weighting)	Yes	Yes
Durability of the system (no need for adjustments at each enlargement)	Yes	No	No
Greater degree of proportionality to population than at present	Yes	Yes	Yes
System easy to understand by the general public	Yes	Yes	No
Easy to apply	Yes	Yes	No

a. This system could also be adapted by applying a small reweighting.

3. the minimum number of member states represented by a qualified majority;
4. whether to maintain the existing 'clusters' of member states;
5. the QMV threshold;
6. the timing of the changeover to the new system.

The way in which each of these parameters was addressed helps explain the outcome arrived at by the Conference.

Reweighting only for Member States Nominating a Second Commissioner?

Two main arguments were put forward to justify reweighting. The first was the need to compensate the larger member states for relinquishing the right to nominate a second national as a member of the Commission. The second was the need to achieve a minimum backing for a qualified majority in terms of population. This legitimacy issue was of direct concern to *all* member states. Even if the larger member states had not been giving up their second member of the Commission, the legitimacy problem would still have needed to be addressed as one of the 'relevant elements' mentioned in the treaty protocol.

Member states with two commissioners argued that the two elements should be addressed separately and additionally, rather than concomitantly. The implication was that only once the legitimacy issue had been addressed could governments begin discussing 'compensation'. However, because both factors were in fact mutually reinforcing, less populous member states argued that no 'double payment' was required, since by addressing the compensation question, the legitimacy issue would take care of itself.

The fact that the demographic backing of a qualified majority was a matter of common concern could be used to justify some form of 'generalized' reweighting, that is, adjusting downwards the weighting of every member of the Council before reweighting the largest member states. Suggestions were made early in the Conference sounding out such approaches, for example, by doubling all member states then subtracting one vote from each. The effect of this would be to raise the minimum population threshold. It would also reweight each member state (except Luxembourg) to all the others, while preserving the existing clusters.

Sweden suggested a 'generalized' reweighting which adjusted the weighting of all members of the Council relative to one another by taking the square root of the population of each member state (rounded to the nearest million, and multiplied by an appropriate coefficient (e.g. 2 or 3) then rounded up or down as required (IGC 2000c). Using the square root preserved the degressive proportionality of the system. While offering the advantage of an objective means of categorizing new member states, this model had two major drawbacks. First, as with all 'generalized' reweighting models, it altered the relationship of all members of the Council to each other, in particular (in the Swedish case) by changing the clusters that had been used to date (see below). Second, in the view of the larger member states it failed to provide an adequate level of 'compensation' and would require further adjustment to do so, thereby removing the objectivity from the system. Both of these approaches, however, involved 'downweighting' most member states relative to the largest member states.

In Nice, the final outcome actually involved a generalized reweighting of all existing member states, but for the medium-sized member states, that reweighting was upwards rather than downwards. This was done by taking as a basis a doubling of the existing votes and giving two additional votes each to Belgium, Greece and Portugal (twelve votes each), two additional votes to Sweden and Austria (ten votes) and one additional vote each to Denmark, Finland and Ireland (seven votes). These concessions were made not as part of the process of seeking a particular 'legitimacy level' for a qualified majority, but as a concession to less populous member states in order to water down the overall size of the reweighting proposed for the larger member states in the initial models tabled by the French presidency.

The Size of the Reweighting
As far as the demographic element was concerned, if a commonly agreed minimum 'legitimacy' level for popular backing of any QMV decision in the Council could be agreed, a quick arithmetical calculation would suffice in order to determine how many extra votes should be allocated to the larger member states to achieve that objective. However, no such agreed 'legitimacy' level existed, although the general view was that the figure should probably not be much lower than the current 58%.

The second element (i.e. compensation for abandoning the right to nominate a second commissioner) belonged to the realms of pure politics. It might have been theoretically possible to construct an objective price for the head of a commissioner. One argument ran as follows: when Spain joined the Union it received two commissioners, but 20% fewer votes than the largest member states; therefore one commissioner is worth 20% of the starting basis for applying any compensation element to the reweighting. In reality, though, a commissioner would be worth whatever heads of government in Nice decreed he or she should be worth!

In the final vote weighting table, the most populous member states have received 29 votes (i.e. doubling the existing voting weights and adding 9), while Spain received 27 (i.e. double the existing votes plus 11). The special case of Spain is explained below. The adjustments agreed at Nice (combining the compensation and demographic elements) have managed to preserve the minimum population level in EU-27 at just above 58%, equivalent to the current level. However, this is subject to application of a 62% minimum population threshold (see below).

The Minimum Number of Member States Represented by a Qualified Majority

The system of vote weighting as it existed up to EU-15 always involved at least half of the member states in any qualified majority. In other words, a single voting table managed simultaneously to meet legitimacy in terms of people and states. This had always been an arithmetical consequence of the system, given the low spread of member states, and at no time had it ever been stipulated as a specific criterion. The problem now was that if more than a moderate reweighting was applied to the larger member states, this automatic, in-built condition would no longer be met, because of the larger spread of member states in the Union. In other words, it would be possible to achieve a qualified majority with fewer than half the members of the Council, albeit in the highly improbable event of all the most populous member states voting in favour of a measure, and all the least populous member states voting against.

Certain member states argued that since this had never been an explicit condition for achieving a qualified majority in the Council in the past, there was no justification for introducing such an additional condition now. However, in the latter stages of the negotiation it became a matter of principle for the smaller member states to have such a requirement enshrined in the treaty as a vital element of legitimacy of the system. Moreover, it constituted a political *quid pro quo* for re-weighting the larger member states and would offer an important safeguard.

The initial presidency bid was to turn the requirement around and consider that a qualified majority consisted of a majority of weighted votes unless a majority of members voted against. The reason was to maintain the minimum population represented by a blocking minority as high as possible by discounting abstentions while still achieving a similar political objective in terms of member state legitimacy. However, at the insistence of the less populous member states, the reverse requirement was turned into a positive one, so that a qualified majority when voting on a Commission proposal will expressly require the requisite number of votes to be cast by a *majority* of members.

While potentially representing a further complicating condition in taking decisions in the Council, it represented a fair point of equilibrium, since the member state criterion does not come into play in the reweighting for EU-15, and in EU-27 (as well as in intermediate configurations of the Union) its practical impact is likely to be negligible since the scenario of the thirteen most populous member states voting in favour and the fourteen least populous voting against a particular measure is sufficiently improbable that it can be discounted for all practical purposes.

Clusters of Member States with Similar Voting Weights
Two very different types of issue arose in this context. The first, more 'technical' in nature, related to the need to create new groupings of member states, particularly at the lower end of the table, to take account of the relative size of new member states that did not fit readily into existing vote categories. As an initial step, the extrapolation table (Table 4.3) was doubled in order to allow new categories to be created. However, with the exception of Malta and Romania, the candidate states were in fact slotted into categories with existing member states and those with six or more votes were 'reweighted' (see below).

The second issue was a matter for heads of government: whether the Netherlands (with a population some 50% greater than Belgium) and Germany (with 40% more inhabitants than France) should both be given additional votes in recognition of their size relative to other members in the same group. The greater size of the German population was already reflected in the European Parliament, where Germany's seats

were increased from 87 to 99 following reunification. While understandable in the context of the European Parliament (representation of
the people), the issue of whether Germany should be decoupled in the
Council was not necessarily self-evident given the way in which the
system of vote weighting was constructed. The key question was
whether France would accept a decoupling of Germany, thereby facilitating Belgian acceptance of an additional vote for the Netherlands.
While most of the larger member states appeared fairly relaxed about
such decoupling, for historical reasons it was politically unacceptable to
France. To reconcile that position with the German desire to see its
greater relative size reflected, the following clause was inserted
alongside the Council vote weightings:

> When a decision is to be adopted by the Council by qualified majority, a
> member of the Council may request verification that the Member States
> constituting the qualified majority represent at least 62% of the total
> population of the Union. If that condition is shown not to have been met,
> the decision in question shall not be adopted.

This clause will take effect in 2005 at the same time as the new vote
weightings. In practical terms, it means that in EU-27, Germany, which
will then account for 17% of the EU population (see Table 4.4), will be
able to constitute a blocking minority with any two of the UK, France
and Italy. In other words, with a blocking minority fixed at 91 in EU-27
(see below), the population clause has the same effect as granting four
additional votes to Germany when it forms a blocking minority with
two other large member states.

France's reluctance to allow a clear-cut decoupling of Germany in
the weighting figures in order to preserve the illusion of parity
(although the result achieved is a real decoupling) made it politically
more difficult for Belgium to accept decoupling the Netherlands (13
votes) from the other member states in the category with 12 votes.
Decoupling the Netherlands could be justified on objective grounds,
since this grouping had a greater 'stretch' in population percentage
terms than even the grouping with the largest member states, and the
ratio between the Netherlands' population and its voting strength constituted an acknowledged anomaly. Belgian misgivings could only be
dispelled at the end of the negotiations once further concessions had
been made on European Parliament seats and on arranging that the total
Benelux votes (12 + 13 + 4 = 29) equalled that of the largest member
states. The agreement on establishing Brussels as the venue for official

European Council meetings (see Chapter 8), also helped to secure final agreement.

The QMV Threshold

Once the vote weightings had been fixed, the QMV threshold in terms of votes still had to be determined. This proved to be the most intractable bone of contention. It was impossible to determine at Nice an absolute figure in terms of votes for the QMV threshold for every intermediate configuration of the Union, since it would depend on which candidate states joined the Union in which order. However, two things had to be done at Nice: a threshold for EU-15 in 2005 had to be laid down in the Treaty Protocol alongside the new weightings in the event of no accessions taking place before that date (see Appendix 1.1); and a threshold for EU-27 had to be laid down in the member states' common negotiating position in the light of the vote weightings actually agreed in the final voting table. Given the general state of weariness at 4.20 am at the end of a four-day marathon when overall agreement was reached, a degree of ambiguity inevitably crept into the final outcome.

Two issues had a particular bearing on the threshold. The first was the initial negotiating position of certain larger member states which were endeavouring to secure a blocking minority of three large member states. While this position was not pressed towards the end of the negotiation, it nevertheless played a role in dictating the final outcome in conjunction with the second issue, namely adjustments to accommodate the special case of Spain.

Spain had been identified as a special case in declaration No. 50 attached to the final act of the Amsterdam Treaty (see Box 4.2 above). The Spanish government sought similar treatment to the large member states. The difficulty was that while Spain had the right to nominate two commissioners, it had two fewer votes in the Council than Germany, the UK, France and Italy (eight as opposed to ten). Its population size made it impossible for Spain to lay claim to the same number of votes as the other large member states. So, a solution had to be found placing Spain on an equal footing with the largest member states without awarding it the same number of votes.

There were two possible ways of doing this. One was to set the threshold for EU-27 at such a level that Spain could achieve a similar degree of blocking power as any three of the four largest member states, a position which Spain had argued for throughout the negotiations. However, this would have led to an unacceptably high QMV threshold. The other was to construct a minimum blocking minority of four members in EU-27, and then fix the votes in such a way that *either* three large members, *or* two large plus Spain would be able to form a blocking minority only with the support of the same fourth member. In order for Spain to enjoy similar blocking power to any three of the largest member states, its votes would have to be fixed by subtracting the votes of the state with the lowest number (Malta, with 3) from 29 and adding one, giving 27 votes for Spain. Allocating Spain two fewer votes than the large member states would allow Spain plus Malta plus any two large member states to block, and would require setting the blocking minority at one more vote than the sum of the votes of the three largest member states (i.e. 88 in EU-27).

The constraints created by securing the position of Spain meant that something had to give. That something was the QMV threshold, which for the first time in the Union's history would be pushed above 71.5%. Any decrease in the overall number of votes for the most populous member states or, conversely, increase in voting strength for the less populous member states would inevitably raise the QMV threshold. Both occurred. Reducing the vote weightings for the largest member states to 29 while reweighting upwards all member states with six votes or more would raise the QMV threshold to 74.78% for EU-27 if the blocking minority was maintained at 88.

The consequences of these movements provoked a reaction, particularly from Belgium, Portugal, Finland and others, who feared that the rising QMV threshold would result in more difficult decision-making after enlargement because of the higher requirement facing other Council members in building coalitions. The compromise solution was the declaration agreed at the end of the meeting regarding the level of the QMV threshold and the number of votes for a blocking minority (cf. Appendix 1.3), which reads:

> Insofar as all the candidate countries listed in the Declaration on the enlargement of the European Union have not yet acceded to the Union when the new vote weightings take effect (1 January 2005), the threshold for a qualified majority will move, according to the pace of accessions, from a percentage below the current one to a maximum of 73.4%. When all the candidate countries mentioned above have acceded, the blocking minority, in a Union of 27, will be raised to 91 votes, and the qualified majority threshold resulting from the table given in the Declaration on enlargement will be automatically adjusted accordingly.

During the process of enlargement, the QMV threshold should initially be reduced to below the current level, then increased to 73.4% of votes until EU-26, depending on the number of acceding states. When all candidate states had acceded in EU-27, the threshold for the blocking minority would be 91.

The convoluted wording of the declaration on the threshold and the blocking minority was the result of calculations being undertaken by delegations on the basis of the weighting table before incorporating the final agreed weighting changes. The table setting out the Union's common negotiating position in the declaration on enlargement (see Appendix 2.2) was not, however, amended at the same time, which explains why the blocking minority threshold in that table remains at 88 (i.e. the QMV threshold is 258). However, retaining the figure of 88 for the blocking minority in the table in the declaration on enlargement in theory allows a much greater negotiating margin in the accession negotiations. The treaty itself allows a threshold to be fixed at a figure of up to 74.78%, because Article 3(2) of the Protocol (see Appendix 2.1) states:

> At the time of each accession, the threshold referred to in the second subparagraph of Article 205(2) of the TEC…shall be calculated in such a way that the qualified majority threshold expressed in votes does not exceed the threshold resulting from the table in the Declaration on the enlargement of the European Union included in the Final Act of the Conference which adopted the Treaty of Nice.

The declaration on the QMV threshold, although a purely political rather than a legally binding statement, was the final piece of the political jigsaw agreed by heads of government. One interesting point about this declaration is that Spain accepted a figure for the blocking minority (91) which actually places it in a more limiting position than the largest member states in terms of finding the broadest possible base to seek blocking allies. Paradoxically, it would have been more interesting for Spain to have sought a figure of 92 (i.e. by reducing the threshold to 254) in order to have the same number of blocking opportunities as the largest member states.

Fixing the threshold for EU-15 in 2005 also proved contentious (see Table 4.7) in the light of the agreement that had been reached by heads of government. While this figure will probably be purely academic in practice, the threshold was important for two reasons. First, for the Union in general, it would constitute a starting point for negotiations on the threshold in each treaty of accession. Second, for Spain in particular, it was vital to demonstrate that its position in EU-15 in terms of the logic of Ioannina had improved as a result of Nice. Spain accordingly sought a QMV threshold fixed at 170. Many delegations argued that the figure should be 168, since that would be the level immediately below the existing threshold of 71.26%. However, with a blocking minority of 70 (which would result from a threshold fixed at 168), Spain would have obtained no improvement over its current position, since it would still have had to seek two large member states in order to constitute a blocking minority of three Council members. In line with the logic of Ioannina, Spain considered that it should be able to constitute a blocking minority of three along with one large member state and one member state with 12 votes, which would require fixing a blocking minority of 68 and a QMV threshold of 170. Striking an acceptable compromise involved fixing the QMV threshold at 169 and the blocking minority at 69: while this figure is very slightly higher than the current QMV threshold (71.31%), it is the figure which is arithmetically the closest to it. It also allows Spain to present the outcome as an improvement (even if not quite Ioannina) since it would be in a position to form a blocking minority with any large member state plus the Netherlands.

While there is therefore a discernible logic in what has been agreed, understanding it requires some constructive piecing together, as well as a grasp of European history! Nevertheless, the actual level at which the QMV threshold is set in future will depend on the numbers of member states acceding to the Union with each wave of accessions, bearing in mind the political content of the declaration on the level of the threshold. This is the institutional issue that is most likely to give rise to tough negotiations among member states at the end of each accession negotiation.

The Timing of the Changeover to the New System

Because of the linkage to the size and composition of the Commission, it was agreed that the changeover to the new system would occur in January 2005 at the same time as the shift to one commissioner per member state, as stated in Article 3 of the protocol on enlargement annexed to the treaties. Table 4.7 illustrates the weighting of votes in the Council agreed by heads of government, which will be applicable from 1 January 2005 for the current fifteen members of the Union (see

Appendix 1.1, Article 3). As far as the candidate states are concerned, their vote weightings will be fixed in the treaties of accession. The declaration accompanying the Protocol attached to the Nice final act sets out the common negotiating position of the fifteen member states with the candidate states, including the vote weighting table for EU-27 (see Appendix 1.2 and Table 4.8).

Table 4.7: Council vote weightings for EU-15 from 1 January 2005

Members of the Council	Weighted votes
Germany	29
United Kingdom	29
France	29
Italy	29
Spain	27
Netherlands	13
Greece	12
Belgium	12
Portugal	12
Sweden	10
Austria	10
Denmark	7
Finland	7
Ireland	7
Luxembourg	4
Total EU 15	237

For their adoption, Council acts require at least *169 votes in favour cast by a majority of members.*

Total votes = 237	Votes	% Votes	Minimum number of members	Minimum % of population
Qualified majority	169	71.31	8	59.93[a]
Blocking minority	69	29.11	3	13.80

a. This figure indicates the minimum population represented by a qualified majority resulting from the application of the voting table. The actual minimum
population figure under Article 205(4) is 62% if invoked by any member of the
Council.

Table 4.8: Council vote weightings for EU-27 agreed at Nice[a]

Members of the Council	Weighted votes
Germany	29
United Kingdom	29
France	29
Italy	29
Spain	27
Poland	27
Romania	14
Netherlands	13
Greece	12
Czech Republic	12
Belgium	12
Hungary	12
Portugal	12
Sweden	10
Bulgaria	10
Austria	10
Slovakia	7
Denmark	7
Finland	7
Ireland	7
Lithuania	7
Latvia	4
Slovenia	4
Estonia	4
Cyprus	4
Luxembourg	4
Malta	3
Total EU-27	345

Council acts shall require for their adoption at least *255 votes in favour cast by a majority of members.*

Total votes = 345	Votes	% Votes	Minimum number of members	Minimum % of population
Qualified majority	255	73.91	14[b]	58.29[c]
Blocking minority	91	26.38	4	11.61

a. The weighting table was constructed by doubling the votes contained in the extrapolation table (Table 5.3) and applying certain technical adjustments in order to produce more homogeneous categories of member states with similar voting weight (Latvia, Slovenia and Estonia, 4 votes; Malta, 3 votes). The votes of the most populous member states were increased from 20 to 29. Further adjustments were made to take account of the objective situations of the Netherlands, as well as the special case of Spain. Reweightings were also applied to the groups of member states in the above table with 7 votes (+ 1), 10 votes (+ 2) and 12 votes (+ 2).

b. Without the requirement for a majority of member states, it would be theoretically possible to constitute a qualified majority with 13 member states.

c. This figure indicates the minimum population represented by a qualified majority resulting from the application of the voting table. The actual minimum population figure under Article 205(4) may be raised to 62% if invoked by any member of the Council.

The Realities and Illusions of Nice on Vote Weighting

It is difficult to escape the feeling that while the outcome at Nice on vote weighting represented a satisfactory outcome for all negotiating parties in terms of achieving their own political objectives, somehow the Union as a whole lost out. It was a feeling shared by many who participated in the exercise. The larger member states achieved their goal of compensation for abandoning the right to nominate a second commissioner through a moderately substantial reweighting. Germany's size was recognized by enabling it to form a blocking minority of three with any two other large member states (in a somewhat less than transparent manner). Spain found itself in many respects on a similar footing to the large member states, although not exactly the same footing. The Netherlands achieved its long-standing objective of increasing its voting weight. All of the current member states achieved some measure of upgrading, with the exception of Luxembourg, although the Benelux states collectively have as many votes as a large member state (29). The less populous member states achieved a political safeguard for their interests since no decision can be taken without their collective consent, since the treaty now stipulates expressly that a qualified majority requires the votes of at least half of the members of the Council. In other words, everyone went home with a presentable result.

However, what will the impact be on Union decision-making? The attentive (and puzzled!) reader may by now be wondering what on earth the difference is between the simple vote reweighting coupled with member state and population 'safety nets' agreed at Nice, and a 'weighted' dual majority system based on a majority of members and the two vote weighting tables illustrated in Table 4.5. The answer, in short, is not a lot, except that the weighting range agreed in Nice goes from 3 to 29 and does not include an additional weighting table from 1 to 170. This demonstrates that two approaches (dual majority and reweighting), often opposed as different concepts in the negotiations on Council vote weighting, are in fact variants of one and the same system attempting to reconcile both a member state and a population element —that is, a Union of states and a Union of peoples.

However, in endeavouring to reflect fully the duality of the Union, heads of government resorted to a conservative, DIY approach by simply grafting a 'population' and a 'member state' element onto the existing system. Some have accordingly dubbed this a 'triple majority' system, in which three separate conditions need to be met in order to achieve a qualified majority:

1. a majority of weighted votes;
2. a majority of members of the Council;
3. a majority representing at least 62% of the Union's population.

Given the need to fulfil three separate conditions as well as meeting a higher QMV threshold as the Union expands, the final outcome is complex, difficult to explain and undoubtedly runs counter to the general desire at the start of the negotiations *not* to make Council decision-making more difficult. The Commission, the European Parliament and many commentators have been critical of the outcome for these reasons. Moreover, there is the further technical complication of how to verify the population criterion. Since it is expressly stipulated in the treaty as a verifiable condition for adopting legally binding acts, it seems inevitable that the Council will at some point need to adopt a decision containing a user-friendly population table similar to Table 4.4 to be used alongside the vote weighting table laid down in Article 205 of the treaty.

However, despite misgivings about the complexity of the voting system, when one moves from the abstract and hypothetical to the practical, the picture is much more positive than the above analysis might suggest.

The requirement for any qualified majority to be composed of half of the members of the Council, although an essential point of principle which had to be written into the treaty to secure agreement, can for all practical purposes be disregarded. The extreme configuration required for this condition to come into play as the determining factor for or against a decision (all of the most populous member states in favour and all the least populous against) is theoretically possible but totally implausible in practice. The Union just does not work like that.

As far as the population clause is concerned, the fact is that qualified majorities typically represent well over 62% of the Union's population. In both EU-15 and EU-27 the population clause can only come into play when Germany is in a minority. The actual impact is, however, difficult to determine exactly. In EU-27, the clause can have an impact if three large Member States including Germany are seeking to form a blocking minority. However, if in EU-27 the interests of three large member states are such that they are seeking to constitute a blocking minority, it is highly likely that other states will also share their position. It is somewhat ironic that the *de facto* result of this clause, which is to accord four additional votes to Germany in EU-27, probably goes well beyond what Germany itself would have regarded as a satisfactory outcome in terms of additional votes in the vote weighting table. However, if Germany had been given more votes in the vote weighting table this would have assisted the process of building qualified majorities in favour of any decision, whereas concealing the additional votes in the population clause means that they can only come into play in constructing blocking minorities. One interesting avenue for further research will be to assess the political impact of the new vote weighting system in various policy sectors and attempting to measure the real power gain for Germany in the light of the enhanced relative position of both Spain and Poland in the vote weighting table.

It is always an interesting academic exercise to compare whether the outcome of any decisions subject to QMV in previous years would have been different under the new voting system. None of the legislative decisions taken by qualified majority in 1999 would have had a different outcome under the new weighting system. The Commission undertook a study during the Amsterdam IGC which purported to show that had a dual majority system been applied, none of the negotiating outcomes in the Council over the previous three-year period would have been different (Petite 2000). It would, however, be wrong to deduce from such calculations that the nature of the voting system used in the Council is somehow irrelevant. The idea that 'nothing changes' is a static, one-dimensional view based on an *ex-post* analysis. Negotiating in the Council is a dynamic process, in which negotiating behaviour is at least partly conditioned by the negotiators' knowledge of potential winning and blocking combinations and by a sense of what is 'achievable' in a given situation. The qualitative aspects determined by the voting system also need to be factored in. It is in these shifting power coalitions or potential coalitions that a negotiating outcome is achieved. The final voting outcome may have been the same, but there is no guarantee that with a system subject to different voting *powers* the substance of the outcome would have been identical. Macro-level quantitative analyses find it difficult to build in such qualitative factors.

So much for the impact of the new system. However, none of the foregoing *explains* the Conference's outcome on vote weighting. Why would heads of government create such a complex voting system given that they did not intend to make decision-making more difficult? Readers will have noticed one *leitmotif* running through this entire chapter: most of the arguments have been based on marginal situations and extreme configurations of member states. This, more than any other factor, explains the outcome. The starting point for this can be traced back to the Amsterdam IGC, where one of the key issues was whether it would be legitimate to have a qualified majority composed of Council members representing less than 50% of the Union's population. Even if such a scenario could only occur in a highly improbable configuration of member states in a Union with more than 27 members, it was felt that the Union must not have a system that even allowed it as a hypothetical possibility.

In addition to the legitimacy argument, two other striking examples of similar reasoning were used during the Conference. The first was in relation to the number of member states, which was again presented as a legitimizing factor for Council decisions. The second example of marginal reasoning throughout the latter part of the Conference and the endgame denouement was the emphasis on blocking minorities rather than qualified majorities. The predominant attitude was not 'how can my votes be made to count most effectively to attain a qualified majority', but 'how can I best ensure that my votes can block decisions that might be contrary to my national interest'. There are two reasons for this. First, a solution for the special case of Spain required entering into the logic of Ioannina, which was a logic based on blocking minorities. The second and more fundamental point is that after enlargement the Council will become an unknown quantity, and faced with uncertainty about the negotiating dynamic in EU-20, EU-25 or EU-27, member states preferred to take the most conservative approach available.

Moreover, in a negotiation where public presentation mattered as much as substance, false problems can become real presentational problems. This underscores the view that semantics and presentation rather than objectivity and rationality drove this politically charged negotiation.

The fact that a member state requirement has now been explicitly written into the treaty, and that a reweighting of the current system has been combined with a population threshold, serves to demonstrate that the different weighting options considered were in reality variants of the same system rather than opposing systems. The Nice system can be described as a 'reweighting', generally advocated by larger member states at the outset, or a 'dual majority' system advocated by many less populous states, or a hybrid blend of the two. Take your pick according to what your audience wants to hear!

Given the real advantages that many Council members (not least Spain and Poland) have acquired under the new system, it is difficult to see where any incentive for change will come from in the future. Although three of the system's basic parameters (i.e. the new weightings, the member state criterion and the population safety net) now appear to be written in stone, there is one crucial element that will remain negotiable: the level of the QMV threshold. This will become a key institutional battleground in each treaty of accession, as heralded in the declaration on the threshold. While it is impossible to speculate on how this declaration will be applied in future negotiations in changed political circumstances, what actually happens to the threshold in practice will depend to a large extent on the comfort level of member states in predicting negotiating outcomes in the new enlarged Union, and the level of security they accordingly feel they need to retain in terms of blocking power in the Council. This allows at least some cause for cautious optimism.

5 |

Extending Qualified Majority Voting

Qualified majority voting (QMV) means taking decisions in the Council by applying the system of weighted votes just described in the previous chapter. It is one of three ways in which the Council takes decisions, the other two being unanimity (all members approving or abstaining) and simple majority (a straightforward majority of members of the Council) which applies mainly for procedural matters. Simple majority is in fact the default rule unless the treaty provides otherwise, which in most cases it does. Treaty articles which contain a legal basis for action specify the voting rule to be used. Following successive IGCs, each of which has resulted in an extension of qualified majority voting to a greater or lesser extent, QMV already applied at the start of the Nice IGC to most decisions taken in the Council. Member states were therefore staring into a chocolate box where all the soft-centres had long been snapped up, with only the more unpalatable hard ones left at the bottom.

QMV was undoubtedly the issue in which the Conference invested most time and effort at the Preparatory Group level. There were two reasons for this. First, an ambitious outcome (or lack of it) would be one of the main yardsticks for measuring the Conference's political success or failure in terms of efficiency. This was because the *prima facie* case for greater recourse to QMV was compelling. Given the arithmetical fact that the likelihood of deadlock increases with the number of member states, failure to secure a reasonably ambitious outcome would be interpreted as both an unwillingness to address the threat of decision-making grinding to a standstill in key areas and of waning commitment to enlargement. Second, the issues involved were complex and included a number of politically sensitive matters. Legal clarity of drafting was a prerequisite if QMV was even to be contemplated for some more sensitive policy areas. The days of constructive ambiguity, which has proved useful in helping drive forward development in sensitive policy areas, are now past, reflecting a broader demand by national parliaments and the general public to know what precisely they are buying with each new treaty.

What of the impact of qualified majority voting on Council decision-making? Some academics, based on a detailed statistical analysis, have put the case that recourse to qualified majority voting has had little measurable impact on the Council's decision-making output (Golub 1999, 2000). Actual recourse to a vote in the Council tends to be infrequent. For example, out of 132 legislative measures adopted in 1999 subject to qualified majority voting, a vote was only actually registered on 28 of them, four of which only resulted in abstentions. Even in adopting the 280 or so directives necessary for the creation of the single market, consensus was achieved on 260 of them (Barnier 2000). However, this does not mean that the impact of QMV is marginal. First of all, the present cannot be extrapolated into the future. What works with fifteen member states will not necessarily do so in a Union of 27 where consensus will necessarily be more difficult to achieve. Second, decision-making effectiveness and, arguably, the quality of legislation are both enhanced through the negotiating dynamic generated by virtue of the very existence of QMV in a particular area as a result of what Weiler terms 'the shadow of the vote' (Weiler 1999). It provides a strong incentive for delegations to make concessions without actually resorting to a vote. It encourages the Commission to contemplate amendments to its proposals as part of the process of compromise building. Finally, in certain sectors, such as agriculture or the budget, votes tend to be threatened or used as a matter of course, since reaching a qualified majority is usually the cut-off point at which negotiating stops because any further concessions are likely to be financially costly. Cost containment in any sector involving significant financial outlays is best served by QMV; unanimity inevitably increases the cost of side-payments to secure adoption of a particular measure (see, for example, Council 1999b, para. 44).

Despite these compelling arguments, QMV has, over the years, been something of a bogey word. The first transition to QMV in the mid-1960s prompted the French empty chair policy which resulted in the Luxembourg agreement (Teasdale 1999). It is also a concept with which successive UK Conservative governments have felt uneasy, although that did not stop them agreeing to significant extensions of QMV in 1986 and 1992 to secure and consolidate the internal market.

Three main arguments are often put forward for opposing an extension of QMV: expansion of the Community's powers, loss of sovereignty and loss of legitimacy. However, in some respects, the arguments are misleading or misplaced and, on closer examination, are somewhat less convincing than they appear at face value.

Expansion of the Community's Powers

The first argument is that extending QMV amounts to an extension of the Community's powers. This misconceived view arises from confusion about the nature of the Community. The Community operates on the principle of conferred powers as stipulated in Article 5 of the EC Treaty (Dashwood 1997). The powers conferred under the treaty establish the limits for action by the Community; the institutions can therefore only act insofar as they have the power to do so under the treaty. The decision-making procedure used to exercise the powers given to the Community cannot alter their scope. Therefore switching from unanimity to qualified majority voting does not imply a change in Community powers. Discussion on some issues, however, such as the Common Commercial Policy (Article 133) highlighted difficulties in distinguishing clearly between an extension of the Community's powers, exercising potential powers which already exist under a particular treaty provision, and an extension of QMV. It is of course perfectly possible to agree to extend the Community's powers as part of the treaty revision process, but this is an entirely separate operation. For the Nice IGC, all delegations shared the basic starting premise that any extension of QMV had to be carried out within the limits of existing powers, especially where treaty articles were substantially rewritten. This was primarily to avoid the need for referenda in certain member states. More generally, even where the Community is given new powers to act in a particular area, it is misleading to portray that as a 'loss of powers' for member states, since this suggests that they no longer have any say in exercising them. The powers pooled in the Community are, however, exercised collectively through the Union's institutions (by national government ministers in the Council and directly elected Members of the European Parliament) in which all member states have a stake. It is perfectly legitimate to argue that relinquishing *de jure* sovereignty by pooling powers in this way can paradoxically enhance a State's *de facto* sovereignty (Patten 2000).

Loss of Sovereignty

The second argument is that recourse to QMV is tantamount to a loss of sovereignty, with sovereignty meaning the ability of an individual member state to defend and articulate its interests in the Union. This argument is typically deployed to resist removal of a member state's ability to veto measures which its government deems to be contrary to its national interest for political or constitutional reasons. On this latter aspect, the need to retain unanimity on matters of a constitutional or quasi-constitutional nature linked to the *sui generis* nature of the European Union is unquestioned by the Commission or any member state (see Appendix 2.3), even those advocating wholesale extension of QMV. The real issue therefore is whether removal of a member government's veto for politically sensitive measures undermines a member state's sovereignty, either because it would run counter to particular national interests or because it involves issues which are deemed crucial in determining voters' domestic political choices. While it is undeniably true that QMV no longer allows an individual government to block any measure it disagrees with, it is not self-evident that this equates to a loss of sovereignty. In an IGC package-type negotiation, an assessment has to be made about whether the economic and political cost of losing the ability to block in one sensitive policy area is compensated by gaining easier decision-making in other areas, where failure by the Union to decide may be equally or even more damaging to a particular State's national interest than the risk of facing unpalatable decisions in the specific area in question. In weighing up these factors, governments must have a degree of confidence in the system's ability to deliver. The dynamics of Council negotiation are as much about co-operation as conflict (Hayes-Renshaw and Wallace 1997). Even where QMV is the voting rule, there is a natural tendency for Council members to seek consensus if possible when confronted with intractable political problems. All member state governments know full well that they may find themselves in a minority on specific issues and would expect some understanding when confronted with difficult political choices. It may be that QMV on all non-constitutional policy matters is always desirable, since the overall balance of gain for the Union will be greater than member state governments retaining the power to block. However, member states, even within a 'club' such as the Union with its well-established rules and conventions, can and do make assessments which lead them to identify certain policy matters for which their interests are best served by retaining unanimity. While the number of such areas are relatively few, they tend to be those which feature prominently in domestic political agendas (such as taxation and social security), in which some governments wish to retain maximum room for manoeuvre in making domestic political choices. By the same token, they are also deemed to be areas where action by the Union is both logical and necessary, particularly in the context of securing and maintaining an effective internal market.

Loss of Legitimacy
Third is the argument that QMV results in a loss of legitimacy of Council decisions. Legitimacy in the Union derives mainly from two sources: directly elected governments taking executive and legislative decisions in the Council (or the European Council), and a directly elected European Parliament co-deciding legislation with the Council and scrutinizing the Commission with the power of censure. Scrutiny over the performance of national governments in the Council can only be exercised via national parliaments on an individual basis, since the Council is not collectively accountable to the European Parliament. As long as unanimity is applied for Council decisions, national parliamentary scrutiny can (in theory at least) be exercised over each individual government's decisions in a particular area. Once QMV is introduced, the fact that individual governments may be outvoted on specific issues is seen by some as undermining the legitimacy of such decisions, because national parliaments can no longer exercise the same degree of scrutiny. However, as a point of general principle, and leaving aside theoretical questions about the boundaries of polities in which majority voting can legitimately be applied, the concept of majority voting, which is central to any democratic system, does not necessarily render decisions any less legitimate provided the system is accepted as fair and no member government is likely to find itself in a permanent minority. Indeed this never happens in practice. More specifically, a partial response has been found by giving greater powers to the European Parliament, which, since the entry into force of the Amsterdam treaty, has a genuine co-legislative role alongside the Council in most legislative matters (see Chapter 6). However, as far as the Council is concerned, this only accounts for part of its work, the rest of which resembles that of a national executive or government. This is not to say that there is no case to answer, only that the case should not be overstated. A legiti-

macy gap issue does exist regarding the accountability and scrutiny of the Council and the European Council, which cannot simply be addressed by giving the European Parliament more powers.

These are important constitutional questions for the Union and which were not examined as such during the IGC, other than being marshalled as arguments in favour of or against various positions. A substantive political examination of these issues is likely to be taken up in the course of preparation for the next IGC in 2004. Some of these questions are considered further in Chapter 9.

Devising an Effective Methodology

General Approach

The general presumption was that extending qualified majority was a 'good thing' in the context of enlargement, despite initial reluctance by certain member states to mention this issue explicitly on the agenda at Cologne. However, the first problem to address was one of method: which approach should the Conference follow in order to guarantee maximum success at Nice? As for all package negotiations in the Union, questions of form, presentation and method matter as much as questions of substance and play an important role in conditioning the final outcome. At the outset two basic approaches were put forward: the first was a case-by-case approach, which involves considering each individual article on its merits. Advocates of this approach argued that it would allow a detailed assessment to be made of the ramifications of moving to QMV for specific areas, and that whatever approach was followed, the Conference would inevitably end up undertaking an examination of each provision individually, with the burden of proof lying with those seeking a move to QMV. The major drawback of starting with this method was that it was likely to elicit a host of objections on each provision proposed as a candidate for QMV. The second suggested approach would involve assuming that qualified majority voting should be the default rule for decisions in the Council, then seeking to define a limited number of exceptions for constitutional or politically sensitive matters. Some member states and the Commission considered that it was more likely to yield a more politically ambitious outcome by establishing QMV as the rule for decisions in the Council. Either a case by case examination of possible exceptions could be undertaken or certain rules regarding such exceptions could be established, thereby placing the burden of proof on those seeking to justify exceptions to the QMV rule. However, this approach was criticized for being somewhat artificial, given the openly acknowledged fact that a fairly extensive number of exceptions would need to be provided for, including a number of constitutional, quasi-constitutional or organic provisions (see Appendix 2.3) not to mention a significant number of politically sensitive ones.

Since neither approach was likely to constitute an acceptable basis for taking work forward, a pragmatic half-way house had to be found. Building on the approach originally outlined in the Finnish presidency's report to the Helsinki European Council (Council 1999d), the Portuguese presidency lumped provisions together into the following five categories for which a convincing case could be put forward for shifting all provisions in each category to QMV:

- *Provisions associated with the functioning of the internal market.* Given that the general rule for internal market provisions was already QMV, provisions closely linked to the operation of the internal market could logically and justifiably be considered as candidates for a move to QMV.
- *Provisions related to the Community budget.* Provisions involving implementation of the budget (e.g. the financial regulation) or creating a legal basis for spending programmes to support member states' action could be shifted to QMV to ensure consistency between the voting rules on legislative substance and on the budgetary procedure.
- *Provisions which could be regarded as institutionally anomalous*, such as those involving codecision with the European Parliament and unanimity in the Council, and those allowing for the possibility of a QMV decision to be appealed to the European Council for a unanimous decision.
- *Appointments* of members of EU institutions or bodies. Given the risk of unanimity blocking essential appointments within the Union after enlargement, QMV would avoid lengthy and damaging internal wrangling to find consensual candidates for key posts in the Union.
- *Provisions relating to the Union's external relations* where qualified majority voting is applied for adopting internal rules. This would establish parallel procedures for the external and internal treatment of the same subject matter.

This category-based approach drove the initial stages of work during the Portuguese presidency and proved surprisingly productive. It enabled the presidency to identify more than forty provisions which could be neatly slotted into one or other of the above categories. A number of additional provisions which did not fall into any of the above categories were also put forward, in addition to some of the politically more sensitive items described below which were dealt with separately from the outset. From late July 2000 on, the Conference embarked on an examination of the text of each provision in turn in order to determine precise formulations of certain articles in which some drafting changes might be required in order to sustain majority support behind a shift to QMV. By that time, the category-based approach had served its purpose by helping retain a substantial list of more than fifty provisions for a shift to QMV until the latter stages of work.

From September onwards, negotiations entered a tactical phase. It was generally accepted that at the end of the day, many minor or purely tactical objections would disappear in Nice, where heads of government would only raise fundamental difficulties. For a few provisions if it became clear that strong resistance was being encountered by more than five delegations, and no obvious way could be found to get round certain practical objections, they were eventually dropped from the list. However, the number of provisions to be removed from the list had to be kept to an absolute minimum. The presidency had to assess whether the provision had any likelihood of passing in the face of strong political objections from perhaps one or two delegations. At that point, tactical considerations came into play: should a particular item be dropped from the text in order to elicit goodwill from a particular delegation on other points, or should it be retained until a later stage and be abandoned as part of a more specific trade-off involving the delegation(s) concerned? The presidency's aim—responding to delegations' expectations—was to retain as many provisions on this list as possible until the very end of the negotiation, given the inevitable pruning down which would take place in Nice itself.

Approach on Politically Sensitive Articles

The method just described lent itself to articles which could potentially switch to QMV in their entirety by simply changing the voting rule applicable, with little need to amend the drafting of the provision. A different approach was needed for provisions covering politically sensitive areas such as taxation or social policy. It would have been unrealistic to propose a wholesale switch to QMV on these and other sensitive provisions. On most of them, the only prospect of moving forward would be to consider QMV for some carefully circumscribed less sensitive aspects within the scope of the provision. Work could then commence on honing the drafting of the article to refine the content and identify the areas in question. Because of the technical complexity of most of these provisions, a considerable amount of negotiating time was devoted to clarifying the texts and refining successive drafts. While in general terms the overall effort invested yielded only modest results, where progress has been achieved, such as on Article 133, the results went further than expected at the start of the negotiations. Six specific areas are examined in turn.

Taxation (Article 93), Social Security Coordination (Article 42) and Social Policy (Article 137)
In these three areas, considerable time and energy was spent trying to redraft the legal bases in the treaty in order to allow some extension of QMV for less sensitive aspects. Although no realistic expectations of dramatic breakthroughs were harboured for any of them, the outcome in Nice was somewhat disappointing for many member states and the Commission. No changes were made on Articles 42 and 93 TEC, and although Article 137 TEC was repackaged to make its content clearer, the extension of qualified majority voting was much less ambitious than many originally sought.

Article 42 provides a treaty basis for coordination of social security schemes to the extent necessary to ensure freedom of movement for workers. Such coordination is obviously essential in a functioning single market in order to ensure that workers and their dependants are not disadvantaged in terms of social security entitlements and health cover when moving from one member state to another. A substantial body of legislation has been adopted under this provision, despite the unanimity requirement, in particular regulations 1408/71 and 574/72. These regulations require frequent adjustment (they have been amended more than 27 times) as national provisions change and Community instruments need to evolve in order to maintain the beneficial effects for the free movement of workers. Many considered that after enlargement it would become virtually impossible to manage an effective working system subject to 27 vetoes. Moreover, this was also one area where the

Council acted unanimously under the codecision procedure with the European Parliament, thereby both eroding the Council's negotiating margin and undermining Parliament's role as co-legislator. Although the treaty does not foresee harmonization of the different social security systems in the Union (even though portrayed as such by some elements in the media) ensuring effective coordination and compatibility between the different systems inevitably involves touching upon sensitive aspects of social policy. The position of Denmark proved to be crucial, because of its residence based (i.e. non-contributory) social security system, the perceived threat of erosion of social security benefits through EU legislation was high on the domestic political agenda. Part of the reluctance to endorse the euro was no doubt attributable to concerns about the impact of euro membership on the Danish social security system. Despite such a charged domestic political climate, the Danish government was open to contemplating a solution which would allow QMV for any updating or adaptation of benefits or persons covered within the scope of *existing* legislation, but unanimity for any extension of that scope. In Nice, however, despite widespread support for a proposed amendment based on this approach, the UK felt unable to accept as a matter of principle given the political commitment in its government's IGC white paper not to accept QMV in this area.

On taxation, an extremely prudent approach was followed by the presidency. This was based on a rewording of Article 93 to cover both direct and indirect taxation and which retained unanimity as the general rule for both. It defined a very limited and exhaustive list of measures for which the introduction of QMV could be considered (relating to certain technical aspects of indirect taxation including environmental taxes and efforts to combat tax fraud). It made explicit that any of the specific measures to be adopted by QMV could not affect directly or indirectly other aspects of tax policy. The French presidency's proposals were considered too modest by some, including France and Germany, which tabled a more ambitious text towards the end of the Conference. However, it was clear that because of firm objections in principle from three delegations (UK, Ireland and Luxembourg) to any extension of QMV there was little hope of any move to QMV. This was despite last minute attempts to explore locating provisions on preventing and combating tax fraud elsewhere in the treaty, coupled with QMV.

Under Article 137 (social policy), qualified majority voting already applies to a large segment of the Union's social policy. The areas still subject to unanimity under Article 137 are the most sensitive, including social security and the social protection of workers, protection of workers when their employment contract is terminated, representation and collective defence of the interests of workers and employers, including co-determination and the conditions of employment for third-country nationals legally residing in the territory of the Community. Various attempts to divide up these subjects in order to facilitate a shift to QMV for adopting minimum standards on certain aspects encountered strong resistance. Article 137 was nevertheless simplified to make it easier to read. In all areas other than those mentioned above an extension of QMV has been foreseen for so-called 'soft' measures, that is, those designed to encourage cooperation between member states through initiatives aimed at improving knowledge, developing exchanges of information and best practices, promoting innovative approaches and evaluating experiences. A provision on modernizing social protection systems was added. The treaty also allowed for the possibility of a Council decision by unanimity to render QMV and codecision applicable to the areas where unanimity continues to apply (with the exception of social security and social protection of workers). However, experience to date shows that without automaticity, clauses which foresee a switchover in voting rules are never used.

The difficulty in all three areas was that national provisions on social security, social policy and taxation reflect fundamental preferences of national legislators and governments. Levels of social protection, welfare benefits and taxation are a key plank of governments' political programmes. From the outset, delegations positioned themselves into three broad camps on these questions: those with no particular difficulties and who could accept a move to QMV, those with fundamental problems of principle, and those in the middle ground with political or practical difficulties but open to seeking ways of resolving them either by limiting the scope envisaged for QMV or by seeking a more precise wording of the articles in question. These difficulties ranged from concern about the impact of QMV on the underlying principles of national social security systems and on their financial equilibrium, to those with specific concerns regarding particular types of benefits or specific elements of taxation. Subsequent redrafts sought to secure a partial shift to QMV by identifying certain specific items for QMV, in the hope of carrying those who could accept an ambitious approach, as well as finding a way round the practical difficulties raised by certain delegations. The tactical aim of such efforts was to narrow down the focus of work and identify which delegations maintained objections in principle.

Delegations reluctant to move on points of principle defended the view that unanimity had not prevented the Union from acting when action was justified and necessary in order to ensure the effective functioning of the internal market. While this is true to some extent, and indeed a certain amount has been done on both social security and taxation under unanimity, these achievements have been hard-won and rely on reasonably disposed governments willing to work towards common solutions in the Union. This cannot always be taken for granted.

Article 67 TEC (Visas, Asylum, Immigration and Judicial Cooperation in Civil Matters)

Before Amsterdam, most of these areas fell under the TEU. The decision to include these areas in the EC treaty was one of the major innovations in the Treaty of Amsterdam (albeit subject to opt outs for Denmark, Ireland and the UK). The Amsterdam treaty provided for a five-year transitional period during which the Council would act unanimously (with a few exceptions) and the Commission would share the right of initiative with member states. At the end of that period, the Council would act on the basis of Commission proposals and had the option of taking a unanimous decision in order to provide for all or parts of these areas to move to QMV and codecision. In the light of the guidelines for action on Justice and Home Affairs questions agreed by the Tampere European Council in October 1999, many delegations considered that implementing this programme effectively warranted eliminating the transitional period and deciding already to move a significant portion of Title IV to QMV and codecision.

Initial drafts of a revised Article 67 endeavoured to take account of various sensitivities in this area by providing for an immediate shift to codecision in certain areas and retaining unanimity in the most sensitive areas. Throughout the negotiations on these matters, France indicated that it would have serious constitutional difficulties to make substantial changes in this article as a result of the way in which the French constitution had been amended in order to enable ratification of the Treaty of Amsterdam. Difficulties were expressed by a number of other delegations, resulting in many cross-reservations on different aspects of the presidency draft. Because of these difficulties in principle, the Conference eventually agreed a solution based on four elements:

- The addition of a new paragraph 5 to allow QMV and codecision to apply from entry into force of the Treaty of Nice for judicial cooperation in civil matters (with the exception of aspects relating to family law) and to asylum measures under Article 63(1) and minimum standards for temporary protection measures for displaced persons under Article 62(2)(a), once the Council has adopted Community legislation defining the common rules and basic principles governing asylum.
- A treaty protocol so that measures to ensure cooperation between member states' administrations and between these administrations and the Commission on matters covered by Title IV of the treaty are decided by QMV (without codecision) from 1 May 2004.
- A declaration constituting a solemn political undertaking to move to QMV and codecision for measures for the free movement of nationals of third countries within the territory of the member states for up to three months and measures on illegal immigration and illegal residence, as well as on standards and procedures to be followed by member states in carrying out checks at external borders as soon as agreement has been reached on the scope of the measures concerning the crossing by persons of the external borders of the member states.
- A declaration containing a best endeavours clause for moving some or all of the remaining matters covered by Title IV of the TEC to QMV and codecision on 1 May 2004 or as soon as possible thereafter.

While a declaration covering the latter two points cannot provide the legal certainty of a treaty amendment, its solemn nature and the fact that it has been adopted at the highest political level mean that there is at least a strong likelihood that it will be followed through in 2004. While a higher degree of ambition might have been sought in the light of the Tampere European Council conclusions, the result represented the only compromise possible at this juncture. A clear trend has however been set for the future in taking the first steps to move to QMV and codecison in this important area of Union policy.

Article 133 TEC (Common Commercial Policy)
In most areas where powers are conferred on the Community, both the Community and the member states legislate alongside one another, with

the member states competent to act (in a manner consistent with Community action) on all matters in that policy area where the Community has not acted. The Community did not on day one of its existence exercise completely and fully all the powers conferred on it. It has exercised its powers gradually as and when needed. The result is that a distinction can be drawn between powers which have been actually exercised, and those which, although conferred, have not yet been exercised.

In certain policy areas, however, no room for manoeuvre is left to member states to legislate without conflicting with Community law. In such areas, the Community's powers are said to be 'exclusive' (i.e. the main substance of policy decisions in a particular sector are taken by the Community), as in the case of the Common Commercial Policy under Article 133 TEC.

The powers and legal instruments for the Union to act in international economic relations have changed little in the past forty years. The contrast between the powers available to the Community under Article 133 and the radical transformations which have occurred on the world economic scene is striking. Article 133 before Nice had only limited scope outside the traditional sphere of trade in goods. With regard to services, it only covered arrangements applicable to the trans-frontier supply of services. It did not cover general arrangements covering international trade in services or arrangements concerning investment or most of the questions concerning industrial and intellectual property rights. Areas outside the scope of Article 133 continue to fall within each member state's field of competence, unless covered by specific legal bases elsewhere in the treaty or by a decision under Article 133(5). Under Article 133(5) as amended by the Treaty of Amsterdam, the Community already potentially has general competence for agreements on services and intellectual property, although this competence had never been exercised.

There are two main difficulties with this arrangement. First, who is answerable if the Community is attacked on a matter covered by a mixed Community/member state agreement where the matter falls under member state competence, but the offending member state has not yet adopted the agreement though the Community already has? The second difficulty is the risk of cross-retaliation within the WTO. WTO dispute settlement mechanisms can authorize a third state to take retaliation measures against a member state even in a sector in which competence lies with the Community. It is therefore possible that retaliation measures can affect the Community as a whole when a single member state has broken WTO rules in exercising its national powers. In such a case, the Community and other member states could suffer the consequences of one member state being in breach of its obligations, yet there would be no means within the Union to compel that member state to bring its internal legislation into line with WTO rules.

Opinion 1/94 of the Court of Justice sought by the Commission at the time of the conclusion of the Marrakesh agreements (the agreements which concluded the Uruguay Round trade talks and established the WTO in 1994) ruled that the areas covered by these agreements went beyond the limits of exclusive Community competence under Article 133 TEC and therefore also had to be concluded by the member states. Following unsuccessful attempts to remedy this situation in Amsterdam, there was a widespread feeling that faced with enlargement, efforts now had to be made to ensure that the Community could continue to function effectively, particularly in the WTO. Certain delegations (in particular Finland) were extremely active in pushing for a real shift to include trade in services, intellectual property and investment within the scope of Article 133. The Commission lent strong backing in advocating updating Article 133 in view of the fact that trade in services, investment and intellectual property rights has superseded trade in goods as the major component of world trade.

Article 133 saw the greatest number of options, redrafts and new proposals (no fewer than twelve during the Conference) right up to the last minute in Nice. The text finally agreed only appeared late on Sunday evening on the Conference's last day, following intense behind-the-scenes negotiating involving the presidency, the Commission and the Finnish delegation. The process of negotiating Article 133 was hampered in the early stages by the absence of a collective systematic analysis of the problems and issues underlying them. There were three reasons why movement was difficult to achieve early on. First, the presidency, while open to examining a full range of options, was hamstrung to a certain extent by a strong national position against any major shift in QMV for nationally sensitive areas such as culture, audiovisual matters, health and education. Second, some delegations were reluctant to show openness on this area unless significant concessions were forthcoming in other policy areas being examined by the Conference. Finally, the subject matter is legally complex—the new and rather unclear wording of Article 133 bears adequate testimony to this (see Appendix 2.5).

To understand what the Treaty of Nice agreed, Box 5.1 illustrates four types of hypothetical trade agreement and compares the situation prevailing before and after the entry into force of the Treaty of Nice. The Treaty of Nice has essentially done two things as far as trade in services and commercial aspects of intellectual property are concerned:

- it has extended the potential scope of exclusive powers under Article 133 TEC without creating any new Community powers. The Community will now be able to exploit to the full its current powers under Article 133, subject to the provisos mentioned in Box 5.1. Prior to the Treaty of Nice the Community's exclusive powers under Article 133 were limited to trade in goods and cross-border services, although Article 133(5) did allow the possibility of extending the area of exclusive powers to services and intellectual property by unanimous Council decision;
- potential recourse to QMV has been expanded, albeit to an extent difficult to quantify. It will be up to the Commission to exploit to the full the possibilities available under Article 133, and ultimately for the Court of Justice to determine where the precise boundaries lie should any grey areas emerge in the course of day-to-day practice, especially given the unclear wording of the new provisions.

Areas Covered by Article 308 TEC
Within the areas where the Community is empowered to act, it was impossible for the treaty's draftsmen to provide for every foreseeable eventuality in the treaty. There may be cases due to evolving circumstances where the Community might need to legislate in order to achieve one of the treaty's objectives, but where no specific legal basis has been provided. Article 308 is designed for that purpose. There was, however, no question of shifting Article 308 to qualified majority voting given its specific nature as a catch-all provision in the treaty. Experience has shown, however, that frequent use has been made of Article 308 in certain areas, in particular to enact measures relating to financial and technical cooperation with non developing countries, the establishment of decentralized agencies and in the energy sector. The issue was whether repeated use of the Article in these areas warranted the creation of new specific legal bases—without any new transfer of competence to the Community—for which qualified majority voting could be envisaged.

Box 5.1: Diagrammatic illustration of Article 133 as amended by the Treaty of Nice

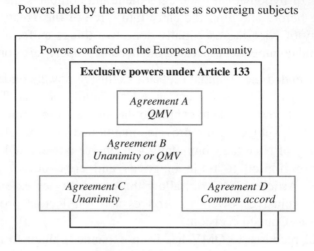

Agreement A

Agreement A covers areas which already fall entirely within the scope of Community competence. Such agreements, as previously, will be concluded by the Council acting by qualified majority.

Agreement B

The Treaty of Nice has widened the scope of exclusive Community competence under Article 133. Agreement B extends beyond the areas where the Community had exclusive competence before Nice, and includes areas within this extended scope of competence in which the Community *has exercised its powers internally*. Such agreements will be concluded by the Council, with the voting rules dependent on the content of the agreement. If the agreement covers matters for which unanimity applies for the adoption of internal rules, unanimity will also apply for conclusion of the agreement (Article 133(5), second subparagraph). Prior to the entry into force of the Treaty of Nice, such agreements are concluded in a similar manner, using the appropriate legal basis in the treaty for the area in question.

Agreement C

Agreement C covers matters which extend into areas where internal powers have been conferred on the Community, but where the Community has not yet exercised those powers. These agreements will in future be concluded by the Council acting unanimously, whereas until the entry into force of the Treaty of Nice, such agreements would have been 'mixed' (i.e. concluded by the Council (unanimously) and the member states by common accord). It should be noted that the Commission has negotiated on behalf of the European Community and the member states for many years (on the basis of a Council mandate), so this does nothing more than codify existing practice for negotiation, but represents a significant step forward as far as the conclusion of agreements are concerned.

Agreement D
Agreement D is a so-called 'mixed' agreement covering areas under both Community and member state competence. As in the past, such agreements will be concluded by both the EC and the member states.

No agreement may be concluded by the Community if it includes provisions which would go beyond the Community's internal powers, in particular by leading to harmonisation of the laws or regulations of member states in an area for which the treaty rules out such harmonisation.

The Council will also act unanimously with respect to the negotiation and conclusion of a horizontal agreement relating to the second subparagraphs of paragraphs 5 (cases where unanimity is required for internal rules or for which powers have not yet been exercised) and 6 (the exceptions listed below). It must be said, however, that the precise scope or meaning of this provision is difficult to interpret and will need to be clarified in practice.

Trade in cultural and audiovisual services, educational services and social and human health services will remain partly under Community competence and partly under member state competence. Agreements on transport are covered by the relevant treaty provisions and not by Article 133.

The Conference considered draft treaty articles on two of these areas (establishment of decentralized agencies and economic, financial and technical cooperation with non-developing countries). In the former case, owing to opposition by the Commission, it became clear that the measure was unlikely to garner sufficient support and was accordingly dropped. The usefulness of adopting all financial and technical cooperation measures (e.g. TACIS, MEDA and so on) with a specific legal basis subject to QMV was widely recognized, however, and resulted in the inclusion of a new Article 181a to this effect (albeit retaining unanimity for association agreements and agreements with candidate states). This article does not include balance of payments support which will continue to be governed by Article 308.

QMV: Modest but Politically Credible Progress

While the final negotiation on QMV in Nice began with a list of well over fifty provisions on the table, a number of them fell by the wayside in the final trade-offs. Initial judgments, as in the aftermath of the Treaty of Amsterdam, however, may have proved to be a little bit harsh. Three factors may at least partly explain why some of the initial assessments were less than enthusiastic. First, two key areas in which both the Commission and the European Parliament had been pushing hard for QMV (social security and taxation) predictably proved to be the most politically difficult, and, despite the time invested, no changes were made because of opposition in principle by a very limited number of delegations. Second, on social policy the QMV gains are meagre (for the reasons outlined above) when juxtaposed with the ambitions of the European Social Agenda which was one of the central themes of the Nice European Council. Third, the European Parliament was critical about the lack of an automatic link between shifting legislative matters to QMV and introducing codecision.

Underlying negotiations on QMV, as on a number of other subjects, conservatism on the part of member states about relinquishing the right to say 'no' for certain measures was undoubtedly fuelled by the fact that a Union of 27 is an unknown quantity. Despite this, however, the Conference has probably done as much as was realistically possible and has even achieved more than anticipated in certain respects. The outcome in the Treaty of Nice will help ensure that decision-making can remain effective after the Union enlarges for the following reasons:

- As Appendixes 2.1 and 2.2 show, the Union has abandoned unanimity on around forty treaty provisions (counting varies depending on what one terms a 'provision'). Unlike Amsterdam, the Treaty of Nice introduced virtually no new provisions, so this shift to qualified majority voting related almost exclusively to existing treaty articles. By way of comparison, the Treaty of Amsterdam only succeeded in shifting around eight existing treaty provisions to QMV! While quantity is not the sole yardstick and quality certainly matters, the result at Nice means that it is possible to affirm that qualified majority voting is the procedure used for most decisions taken on a day to day basis in the Council. Bearing in mind that it is generally accepted as desirable that most of the provisions listed in Appendix 2.3 should remain subject to the unanimity requirement, future negotiations on extending QMV will necessarily be limited to the areas listed in Appendix 2.4.

- The number of qualifications or provisos written into certain provisions in order to enable a shift to QMV was relatively limited, and in most cases their acceptance was arguably better than refusing outright to contemplate any shift to QMV for the areas in question. Delegations in general were conscious of the need to retain a reasonably high level of ambition and consequently preferred to seek solutions either by removing only the most sensitive items or deferring the shift to QMV on around eight provisions. On this latter point a deferred, but automatic, shift to QMV is nothing new in the Union. It means that the decision has already been taken and the changeover is automatic. Deferred application should not be underestimated; indeed, all of the provisions listed in Appendix 2.2 (deferred application of QMV) are unquestionably vital for the effective functioning of the Union after enlargement. This is particularly true for the financial regulation (from 1 January 2007), which is subject to frequent amendment, and for rules on the structural and cohesion funds (from 1 January 2007 or the entry into force of the new financial perspective, if later) which represent the second largest item of EU expenditure. Criticism would certainly have been warranted had no decision been taken on either of these areas.

- As indicated above, the reworking of Article 133, if somewhat complex, nevertheless represents a significant change in both extending the scope of QMV and reducing recourse to mixed agreements (i.e. those also requiring approval by each member state in accordance with their internal procedures in addition to the Community). Had France not held the presidency, it is doubtful whether this outcome could have been achieved. On Article 67, while the outcome is somewhat convoluted, some progress will be made already on entry into force of the Treaty of Nice and by 2004 a further step forward on QMV and codecision will be achieved, even if a significant part is couched in the language of a declaration rather than treaty amendment. However, there is no reason to suppose that these solemn political commitments at the highest level will not be followed through.

- Seven of the QMV provisions relate to appointments to the institutions. While the introduction of QMV for appointments to EU institutions with representatives from each member state (e.g. the Court of Auditors, the Economic and Social Committee and the Committee of the Regions) is arguably somewhat artificial, the important point is that significant inroads have been made in what was previously a no-go area for QMV. In the case of the appointment of the president of the Commission and the Secretary-General of the Council/High Representative for the Common Foreign and Security Policy, the breakthrough is almost revolutionary. Interestingly, the nomination of the president-designate of the Commission under Article 214(2) is the first time that the Council at the level of heads of state or government will act by qualified majority. Since this initial breakthrough has now been made, there is no reason why in the next IGC all appointments should not be made by qualified majority voting.

Each new treaty inevitably represents a step forward in recourse to qualified majority voting; the Treaty of Nice has made a not insubstantial contribution. By any measure, it represents, if not a spectacular advance, at least a credible outcome for the Union faced with the prospect of enlargement. Ambitions inevitably need to be trimmed at the end of an IGC. The next IGC scheduled for 2004 will present an opportunity for making further inroads on unanimity, although that exercise will prove more difficult because of the much more restricted starting baseline in the light of what has been agreed in Nice.

6 |

The European Parliament

The European Parliament represents the peoples of the member states and has always been a winner in IGCs. As the Union's powers have expanded into new policy areas and the process of integration has moved forward with each successive IGC, the European Parliament's powers have grown apace. There is nothing surprising in this; increased powers for the Parliament is seen as a natural corollary to the Union's wider policy reach as a means of enhancing the democratic legitimacy of EU legislation, particularly where QMV is used in the Council (see below). The European Parliament is, however, often mistakenly regarded as the Union's legislature; this is only partly true. This again illustrates the difficulty in trying to understand the Union by drawing analogies between it and national institutional contexts. It is more usual to think of the Union as having a 'legislative process' rather than a 'legislature' as such. Legislative decisions are made by the Council or, in most cases, by the Council acting in tandem with the European Parliament under the codecision procedure, involving a process of two readings in both the Council and the European Parliament (see Corbett, Jacobs and Shackleton 1999 for a detailed description). The Commission also plays a key role as the initiator of legislative measures and acts as a facilitator throughout this process, using its institutional prerogatives. Given the Parliament's increasingly important legislative role, which is bound to increase in future, its ability to function efficiently matters.

One important question impacting on the European Parliament's effectiveness is its overall size. While other equally important factors determining the Parliament's effectiveness are being addressed as part of the process of internal reform to prepare for enlargement, its size and the allocation of seats in each member state are a matter to be decided in the treaty. This encapsulates the two types of issue relating to the Parliament that had to be addressed in the Treaty of Nice. The first, directly linked to enlargement, was the allocation of seats. The Treaty of Amsterdam, in accordance with the Parliament's own proposal, placed a cap of 700 on the number of Members of the European Parliament (MEPs) in order to keep the Parliament to a manageable size. The Conference had to consider on what basis to allocate a reduced number of MEPs to be elected in each member state within the overall ceiling and, indeed, whether to retain the ceiling fixed at Amsterdam. The second group of issues related to the Parliament's legislative role, in particular whether the codecision procedure under which most legislative acts are decided jointly by the Parliament and the Council, should be extended to further policy areas, and whether the nature of such 'codecided' legislative acts should be clarified. The European Parliament's standing before the Court of Justice has also been raised in two significant ways, and some other Treaty changes that affect the Parliament have been made.

Allocation of Seats in the European Parliament

The number of EP seats allocated to each member state was an important political issue for two reasons. First, as co-legislator and one arm of the budgetary authority, the Parliament has real power. Secondly, many emphasized the view that the real political linkage as far as influence in the Union was concerned was between Council vote-weighting and the allocation of EP seats rather than the number of Commissioners; while MEPs do not represent governments, there is still a marked tendency for divisions in the Parliament to occur along national rather than party political lines. In the view of some member states, the Conference should not result in 'double payment' in terms of both Council votes and MEPs. The proposal made during the Conference by the European Parliament and the Commission for a number of members to be elected on European-wide lists that would be presented to all voters throughout the Union was discounted at an early stage precisely because it would represent an ambitious change in the EP's election system given the Union's current level of integration. It would also result in a further reduction of national seats at a time when member state governments were already being pushed to cut down the number of their MEPs. In some member states, particularly those with federal or devolved constitutions, the need to reduce the number of MEPs could lead to difficult wrangling in determining the internal shareout of these seats.

Approaches Examined by the Conference

At present, the European Parliament has 626 members allocated in accordance with Article 190(2) TEC (see Table 6.1). Germany originally had the same number of members as the other large member states, but its share was increased to 99 after unification. If the current allocation formula used to determine the number of Parliamentarians elected in each member state was extrapolated to candidate countries, the total would grow to 874 in EU-27, a figure universally deemed to be too high for an effective and manageable parliament. A ceiling of 700 had been fixed at Amsterdam with a view to enlargement. The Conference retained this ceiling as a working assumption for most of its work, and accordingly considered options for determining the number of members to be elected in each member state within it. Two main options were tabled at an early stage in the Conference (see Table 6.2): one based on an extrapolation of the present system and applying a linear reduction in order to respect the ceiling of 700, and the other, suggested by the European Parliament, based on allocating seats by applying a key which reflected much more closely the population of each member state.

Table 6.1: Current allocation of EP seats for EU-15

Member states	MEPs	Population (000s)
Germany	99	82165
United Kingdom	87	59623
France	87	58747
Italy	87	57680
Spain	64	39442
Netherlands	31	15864
Greece	25	10546
Belgium	25	10239
Portugal	25	9998
Sweden	22	8861
Austria	21	8092
Denmark	16	5330
Finland	16	5171
Ireland	15	3775
Luxembourg	6	436
Total EU	626	375969

Eurostat population data 2000.

The Treaty of Nice and Beyond

Table 6.2: Two main methods of EP seat allocation proposed to the Conference

Member states	Population (000s)	Option 1 EP method	Option 2 Linear reduction
Germany	82165	104	77
United Kingdom	59623	77	69
France	58747	77	69
Italy	57680	75	69
Spain	39442	52	51
Poland	38654	51	51
Romania	22456	32	35
Netherlands	15864	23	25
Greece	10546	17	20
Czech Republic	10278	17	20
Belgium	10239	17	20
Hungary	10043	16	20
Portugal	9998	16	20
Sweden	8861	15	18
Bulgaria	8191	14	17
Austria	8092	14	17
Slovakia	5399	11	13
Denmark	5330	11	13
Finland	5171	10	13
Ireland	3775	9	12
Lithuania	3699	9	12
Latvia	2424	7	8
Slovenia	1988	6	7
Estonia	1439	6	6
Cyprus	755	5	6
Luxembourg	436	5	6
Malta	380	4	6
Total EU-27	481675	700	700

Option 1 (method proposed by the European Parliament): Each member state would be allocated a minimum of four seats and the remaining seats would be distributed according to a scale directly proportional to the population of each member state.

Option 2 (method proposed by the Portuguese Presidency): The number of seats in each member state would be based on an extrapolation of the current allocation, to which a linear reduction would be applied to respect the ceiling of 700, with a minimum of six seats.

Eurostat population data 2000.

In determining the seat allocation, Article 190(2) TEC also requires that 'the number of representatives elected in each Member State must ensure appropriate representation of the peoples of the States'. This provision is designed to ensure that less populous member states should receive a sufficient number of members adequately to represent the main strands of political opinion in that Member State. However, what this minimum number should be was contentious. Under the current system, Luxembourg has six members, which it considered to be an absolute minimum.

Neither of the two main options on offer was likely to achieve consensus. The linear reduction model based on the current allocation system tended to favour small and medium-sized member states. Supporters of this formula stressed the fact that it already made provision for a proportional representation of population (albeit in degressive form). Some felt that the introduction of an additional element of proportionality could only be justified at a stage of integration in the Union that went beyond current ambitions.

The European Parliament's proposal was based to a much greater extent on proportionality to population. While entirely legitimate as an approach for an institution which represents the peoples of the member states, it presented three major political drawbacks. First, the number of members would be reduced in all existing member states except Germany, which would see its members rise from 99 to 104. Second, it allocated a minimum of four seats rather than the current figure of six. Third, it would drastically reduce the number of MEPs in less populous member states by a third or more.

The presidency's initial attempt to bridge these positions in Nice was to seek an intermediate approach that introduced a greater degree of proportionality to population compared with the present system, without going as far as the system advocated by the European Parliament. Although it represented a median approach between the two proposals on the table, it was rejected by most member states as insufficient. The presidency was then faced with the inevitable; if the cake is not big enough to give everyone a large enough slice, then a bigger cake needed to be ordered. The failure by heads of government to retain the 700 member ceiling agreed at Amsterdam ostensibly for reasons of efficiency has been much criticized. However, in a negotiation constrained by such a narrow agenda, the allocation of European Parliament seats inevitably became one of the few more malleable variables which could be used to create some negotiating room for manoeuvre. If agreement required the 700 ceiling to be breached, it was clear that this ceiling would not hold out for long.

The final seat allocation for EU-27 is set out in Table 6.3. The basic construction of this table is as follows:

1. The minimum number of members required to ensure 'adequate representation of the peoples' is five, the proposed seat allocation for Malta. The number of seats for Luxembourg remains unchanged at six.
2. For the allocation of seats up to the Netherlands, the figures for the linear reduction model have been used (since it favours less populous member states), with the exception of Belgium, Portugal and Greece, which each received an additional two seats as a negotiating concession towards the end of the session in Nice.
3. For the more populous member states, a greater degree of proportionality in relation to population has been introduced, with Germany retaining the same number of MEPs as at present.
4. As a consequence of applying the changes outlined above, the ceiling has been raised to 732. As mentioned above, the ceiling was not viewed as an immovable negotiating parameter but simply the result of applying the various concessions which formed the negotiable elements of the final package.

The fact that the Czech Republic and Hungary, whose population size would normally place them in the same group as Belgium, Greece and Portugal, have received two fewer seats has elicited much comment. This outcome is simply the result of concessions made to the three member states in the same 'group' at the very end of the negotiation. Consequently, heads of government were aware of the seat allocation being decided; it was not a clerical error or a miscalculation. Neither was it some deliberate form of discrimination. Although unfortunate in political presentation terms, the numbers had been explicitly and consciously agreed by heads of government as an integral part of the overall IGC package, so it was impossible to contemplate any change without reopening the whole Nice package. It should be noted, however, that the seat allocation for candidate states is not already fixed in the treaty but forms part of the common position of the member states for accession negotiations. What actually happens in accession negotiations will depend on the circumstances at that time. While such positions are normally offered on a 'take it or leave it' basis given the difficulties in reaching agreement inside the Union, both candidate states concerned have announced publicly that they will seek to correct what they consider to be a technical anomaly in the course of their accession negotiations.

Table 6.3: Allocation of seats in the European Parliament for EU-27 in the Treaty of Nice

Member states	MEPs
Germany	99
United Kingdom	72
France	72
Italy	72
Spain	50
Poland	50
Romania	33
Netherlands	25
Greece	22
Czech Republic	20
Belgium	22
Hungary	20
Portugal	22
Sweden	18
Bulgaria	17
Austria	17
Slovakia	13
Denmark	13
Finland	13
Ireland	12
Lithuania	12
Latvia	8
Slovenia	7
Estonia	6
Cyprus	6
Luxembourg	6
Malta	5
Total EU-27	732

Transitional Arrangements
The Conference accepted early on that it would be impractical to expect sitting MEPs to stand down during their term of office. Similarly, it is unlikely that all twelve candidate states currently negotiating accession treaties will join the Union prior to the next EP elections in 2004. In order to avoid an immediate reduction in the number of MEPs in existing member states to the level agreed for EU-27, Article 2 of the Protocol on the enlargement of the European Union (see Appendix 1.1) allows for the number of MEPs for the 2004 to 2009 parliamentary session to be fixed within the ceiling of 732 on the basis of treaties of accession signed before 1 January 2004. A correction will be made to ensure that as long as the ceiling of 732 is respected, the number of MEPs elected in the existing member states will be corrected up to the current level or as near to it as possible. A *pro rata* correction will also be made for new member states. The actual number will be fixed by Council decision, although this will be a straightforward technical act applying the mathematical formula laid down in the treaty. Any states signing treaties of accession after 1 January 2004 and joining the Union in the course of the 2004–2009 parliamentary session may result in the 732 member ceiling being breached until 2009. At that time, the seat allocation foreseen for EU-27 will be applied for all member states, irrespective of the number of candidate states which join in the intervening period. This means that there may be some uncertainty as to the total number of MEPs during the period 2004–2009, but from 2009 onwards the ceiling laid down in the treaty will apply.

European Parliament's Legislative Role

Extending the Codecision Procedure to New Policy Areas
Pursuing the logic initiated at Maastricht and Amsterdam, the Conference considered to what extent further legislative areas should be subject to codecision. Both the European Parliament and the European Commission took the view that all areas of Community legislative work should be subject to codecision, including the Common Agricultural Policy and texts involving autonomous rules under the Common Commercial Policy. Most delegations were willing to consider some extension of codecision, provided a case-by-case examination was made of each provision and no automatic link was established with the shift to qualified majority voting in a particular area. A number of

delegations argued, conversely, that an automatic link should exist between use of codecision and use of qualified majority voting, given that the process of negotiation between the two institutions is seriously hamstrung if the Council has to act unanimously. The initial list contained in the report by the Portuguese presidency to the Feira European Council (IGC 2000c) contained a number of provisions for which qualified majority voting already applied under the treaty. The final list agreed by the Conference, however, only contained around fifteen provisions for which the Conference had decided to undertake a shift to qualified majority voting (cf. provisions marked with an asterisk in Appendixes 2.1 and 2.2), in view of concerns about possible knock-on effects in more politically sensitive areas of extending the procedure to existing treaty provisions already subject to QMV.

Operation of the Codecision Procedure
The procedure as set out in Article 251 TEC was not amended in the Treaty of Nice. As a result of the changes agreed at Amsterdam, the Council and the European Parliament have been forced to cooperate ever more closely because of the sheer number of co-decided acts which have to be processed and the pressure on both institutions to reach agreement (Shackleton 2000). However there was felt to be no need to amend the procedure itself in Article 251 given the practical arrangements that had been put in place in the Joint Declaration of the European Parliament, the Council and the Commission of 4 May 1999 (EC 1999) and which appeared to be working well.

Legislative Acts and a Hierarchy of Norms
The resultant increase in workload imposed on both the Parliament and the Council led the Conference to consider whether the notion of a legislative act should be clarified in the treaty. This hearkens back to the debate initiated during negotiations on the Maastricht treaty about introducing a 'hierarchy of norms' into the Community legal frame-work by distinguishing between constitutional, legislative, regulatory and administrative rules, and differentiating between the decision-making processes according to the level of the act adopted. The Conference explored a less ambitious form of this idea in a bid to reflect the practice in member states where a distinction is drawn between acts dealing with the essential aspects of a subject covered by a legislative procedure, in which national parliaments are fully involved, and tech-

nical implementing measures under such acts which are usually decided by a lighter procedure. The practical problem is that much codecided Community legislation is extremely detailed and technical in character, for example, measures harmonizing windscreen wiper systems or directives on the ingredients of various types of foodstuffs. The reason is that at the outset, because of concerns about the way in which the Parliament might exercise its legislative powers, member states proceeded to apply a reverse logic when the codecision procedure was introduced at Maastricht and singled out technical and less politically sensitive areas for application of the new procedure, rather than more politically sensitive areas which lent themselves more readily to general legislative principles. Given the positive experience of codecision, the question is whether it is appropriate for the legislator to decide or amend technical specifications in such detail with full legislative procedures. There is a strong case for allowing for better control over the growing workload imposed on the Council and the Parliament by the continual extension of the codecision procedure which would also have the advantage of clarifying the decision making process in the eyes of the Union's citizens.

Both the Portuguese and French presidencies suggested taking as a starting point for defining legislative acts provisions already subject to codecision. Measures adopted by codecision on the basis of these provisions would be legislative acts which would be confined, as far as possible to defining general principles, the objectives and the essential elements of the measures to be taken, to the extent desired by the co-legislators. Detailed implementing measures, the scope of which would be laid down in the legislative act, would be adopted by the Council or the Commission. However, the European Parliament and a number of member states considered that this amounted to a significant shift in the existing balance of power between the Council and the Parliament. They contended that if such an approach were to be followed, the logic should be pursued to its conclusion by agreeing a proper hierarchy of Community acts. Since the idea failed to rally sufficient support, it was shelved for the time being, but appears likely to resurface in preparations for the next IGC.

Cooperation Procedure

Since it was not possible to abolish the cooperation procedure during the Amsterdam IGC because of the political undertaking at that time not to touch any of the treaty provisions related to economic and monetary union, most delegations favoured its abolition this time in the interests of rationalizing and simplifying the Union's decision-making processes. The general view was that the four provisions in question (Articles 99(5), 102(2), 103(2) and 106(2) TEC) were not legislative in nature and that consequently, they should revert to a simple consultation procedure with the European Parliament. However, given the fact that a few member states did not wish to go against the European Parliament's insistence that in the case of two of them (Articles 99(5) and 103(2)) codecision should apply, the cooperation procedure was retained in order to avoid weakening the European Parliament's legislative position.

Assent Procedure
The assent procedure has been extended to cover decisions determining a clear risk of a serious breach of the fundamental principles on which the Union is founded (see Chapter 8). The Parliament has also been given a right of initiative for such determinations. Assent will also apply to decisions to initiate enhanced cooperation under the first pillar in areas subject to codecision (see Chapter 7). Assent has, curiously, been retained for Article 161 TEC (structural and cohesion funds) for which the Conference agreed to move to QMV in 2007 after the next financial framework has been agreed. While Spain and others considered that assent offers the Council a stronger hand, that is debatable, since the assent procedure does not lend itself to the adoption of legislative texts. Codecision appeared to be a more logical choice in the light of past experience of using this article, given that in negotiations during both Delors II and Agenda 2000, a *de facto* codecision procedure was followed for the entire structural fund package (Galloway 1999).

Other Issues Relevant for the European Parliament

Parliament's Standing before the Court of Justice
Responding to two requests by the European Parliament, its standing before the Court of Justice has been improved in two significant ways which place it on an identical footing with the Council, the Commission and the member states:

- Under Article 230 TEC, the European Parliament will be entitled to bring actions on grounds of lack of competence, infringement of an essential procedural requirement, infringement of the treaty or of any rule of law relating to its application or misuse of powers. While some misgivings were expressed on constitutional grounds about according this right to an exclusively legislative body, it was felt that the Parliament would exercise its powers responsibly and that no real risk existed of having a 'third reading' of legislation in Court.
- Article 300(6) TEC has been amended to allow the European Parliament to obtain an opinion of the Court of Justice on whether an agreement envisaged with third states or international organizations is compatible with the provisions of the treaty.

Political Parties at European Level

Article 191 TEC emphasizes the importance of political parties at European level as a factor for integration within the Union. Following a Commission proposal, the Conference agreed to include an operational provision in that article for the Parliament and the Council to lay down the regulations governing political parties at European level, in particular the rules regarding their funding. It was agreed that funding for political parties at European level provided out of the Community budget may not be used to fund either directly or indirectly political parties at national level, and that the provisions shall apply to all forces represented in the European Parliament on the same basis.

Information to the Parliament under Article 300(2) TEC

The amendments made to Article 300(2) TEC (see Chapter 8) have also extended the right for the Parliament to be informed on the establishment of the Community position in bodies that are set up under any agreements with third countries, and that adopt decisions having legal effects. The Parliament's right to be informed was previously limited to association agreements established under Article 310 TEC.

The European Parliament after Nice

Given the significant gains made by the Parliament in previous IGCs, most notably at Maastricht and Amsterdam, it was inevitable that at Nice, in a negotiation deliberately seeking not to alter substantially existing interinstitutional relationships, the Parliament was going to be less than enamoured with an outcome which could never live up to the high expectations set out in its resolution on the IGC, a resolution that in many respects went beyond the Conference's remit (European Parliament 2000). The further extension of codecision to a number of new areas does not alter the institutional balance; it merely follows the natural logic of the process begun at Maastricht although it did not go as far as the Parliament itself had hoped. In addition, the Parliament has made significant gains under Article 7 TEU (clear risk of a breach of fundamental rights by a member state—see Chapter 8) as well as in terms of its standing before the Court of Justice.

On seat allocation, the outcome in Nice, apart from some obvious anomalies, has injected a greater degree of proportionality to population into the allocation system, which represents a move in the right direction for the institution that represents the peoples of the Union. However, the Parliament must be frustrated at the fact that planning any sensible reform of its internal logistics and working methods is rendered more difficult because of lack of certainty about its future size. Having increased the maximum size of the Parliament at Nice, doubts have been raised about whether the new ceiling will hold in future, or whether it will simply be ratcheted up the next time that painful decisions need to be taken on seat allocation. On the other hand, the outcome also demonstrates that, in the eyes of certain member states, maintaining an adequate share of MEPs is seen as important, both for domestic political purposes and for reasons of representation given the Parliament's increased legislative powers.

7 |

Enhanced Cooperation

'Enhanced cooperation' is a term of art that refers to allowing a number of member states less than the full membership to use the Union's institutions and procedures to act collectively on matters covered by the treaties. Like much Euro-jargon, it can mean different things. The term is often used as a generic label describing all types of flexible arrangements found in the treaties which differentiate among member states in the scope and pace of integration. However, it is more commonly used to refer to one particular brand of flexible arrangement, namely co-operation by groups of member states on the basis of 'enabling clauses' originally introduced in the Treaty of Amsterdam.

Flexible arrangements in one form or another have always been a feature of the Union. Examples include transitional periods in treaties of accession, member states with opt outs or moving at different speeds towards full economic and monetary union, the 'opt-outs' (or potential 'opt-ins') for Denmark, the UK and Ireland on visas, asylum, immigration and other 'Schengen' matters, and so-called constructive abstention on CFSP decisions. An array of buzzwords have been devised to describe these arrangements, including 'enhanced cooperation', 'flexibility', 'closer cooperation', 'differentiated integration', 'variable geometry' or 'multi-speed Europe' to cite but a few. These terms are sometimes used interchangeably, though subtle distinctions can be drawn between them. The fact that Jacques Delors and William Hague have found themselves unlikely bedfellows in embracing the idea of more flexibility in the Union, albeit for diametrically opposed reasons, amply demonstrates that it can potentially be viewed as an accelerator for, or a brake on, further integration depending on where the emphasis is put. One of the main problems encountered both at Amsterdam and Nice was the difficulty in conceptualizing different forms of cooperation between member states in and around the Union. This is because no agreement exists among member states about the precise political purpose of developing opportunities for enhanced cooperation in the treaties, although it is generally perceived as a vehicle for fostering further integration. An extensive body of academic literature has helped clarify the concepts (Stubb 1998) and analyse the impact of such arrangements on the Union's past and future development (Philippart and Sie Dhian Ho 2000). Box 7.1 outlines the terminology as generally understood by negotiators on the Treaty of Nice.

Box 7.1: Forms of cooperation between EU member states

In addition to normal action under the treaties, member states may cooperate in any one of a variety of ways. The term 'enhanced' or 'flexible' cooperation in a generic sense is usually only applied to cooperation of the second type described below (i.e. inside the Union's institutional framework):

1. Cooperation *outside* the Union's institutional framework
    (a) Cooperation 'overlooked' by the treaty
         It is sometimes forgotten that the treaties do not prevent any two or more member states cooperating among themselves. As sovereign entities they are free to organize relations between them as they deem fit, provided, of course, the Union's objectives are not undermined and obligations entered into as Union members are fully respected. This ranges from bilateral diplomatic and political agreements (such as the Franco-German Cooperation treaty) to organized forms of cooperation involving a number of member states, sometimes with third states (e.g. Airbus, Eurocorps, European Space Agency, Eurocontrol and so on).
    (b) Cooperation mentioned in the treaty
         Article 17(4) TEU does not preclude closer cooperation among member states within NATO and Article 306 TEC allows for regional unions such as the Benelux to the extent that the objectives of these regional unions are not attained by the treaty. Explicitly mentioning such cooperation in the treaties highlights the fact that they are compatible with treaty obligations. During the Nice IGC, the Conference considered briefly whether cooperation between two or more member states which contributes to the Union's general objectives, even if it takes place outside the institutional framework, should be given some more loose but systematic recognition under the umbrella of the treaty. This idea met with widespread scepticism, mainly because of fears of creeping Union competence.
    (c) Special case of the 'Euro' group
         The 'Euro' group of Finance ministers which meets in the margins of the ECOFIN Council is an example of cooperation outside the Union's institutional framework which is nevertheless closely

linked to the Union's single currency, in which not all member states are yet members. This group was established entirely outside the institutional framework on the basis of the 1997 Luxembourg European Council conclusions. It has been suggested that one of the reasons this arrangement did not anticipate seeking a basis under the enabling clauses in the Treaty of Amsterdam was precisely because they were deemed too constraining and unworkable even before the treaty entered into force.

2. 'Enhanced' cooperation *inside* the union's institutional framework
    (a) 'Pre-determined' or 'pre-defined' enhanced cooperation
         To date, enhanced cooperation in any meaningful form has only actually been realized in areas singled out in the treaty or in treaty protocols for which all the relevant principles, rules and procedures governing that cooperation are spelled out. These types of arrangements, best exemplified by EMU and 'Schengen' matters, are often referred to as 'pre-determined' or 'pre-defined' enhanced cooperation, because the precise area covered is clearly predefined in the treaty itself.
    (b) 'Enabling clause' enhanced cooperation
         Enabling clauses specify general principles, conditions and procedures for allowing a number of member states to cooperate more closely on a case-by-case basis. Unlike pre-determined enhanced cooperation, detailed arrangements would have to be set out in the act establishing the cooperation in question, in particular to define precisely the area in which it would apply. Enabling clauses were introduced into the Treaty of Amsterdam under the EC Treaty and the third pillar (cooperation in police and criminal justice matters).
    (c) Enhanced cooperation by default
         In this case enhanced cooperation is not the result of the desire by a number of member states to move forward, but rather the possibility for member states to 'opt out' on individual decisions. Examples include constructive abstention under the CFSP and the possibility under Article 34(2)(d) TEU for certain conventions on cooperation in police and criminal justice matters to enter into force for a limited number of member states.

Setting the Agenda

The first stumbling block was whether the Conference should be discussing the issue at all. This was the most intractable of the agenda-setting skirmishes. During the Conference's preparatory phase, a split emerged between a majority advocating the status quo, and a number of member states arguing for treaty change. Three arguments were advanced for not including this topic on the Conference's agenda. First, enhanced cooperation might become a red herring diverting political effort from extending QMV. Second, candidate states were likely to (and most did, with the exception of Bulgaria) view with apprehension any treaty changes which might be construed as creating a *de facto* two-speed Europe. Third, as far as the enabling clause provisions were concerned, since they were as yet untried, it appeared premature in the absence of practical experience to contemplate amending treaty text which had barely been in force for a year. Advocates of change on the other hand argued strongly that it was precisely because they had been too rigidly framed that the existing enabling clauses had not been used. The increasing heterogeneity of the Union as a result of enlargement was likely to make unanimity to launch enhanced cooperation impossible to obtain. Rendering them more flexible might also, paradoxically, encourage the Conference's efforts to extend QMV in order to reduce the likelihood of them being used.

Easier access to enhanced cooperation was also seen as the best way of reducing the temptation for member states to develop forms of closer cooperation, including potential 'pioneer' or 'vanguard' groups outside the EU treaty framework mooted in speeches by President Chirac and Joschka Fischer.

In assessing the situation following preparatory consultations, the Finnish presidency reached the conclusion in its report (Council 1999d) that while there was some interest in exploring certain aspects of the treaty provisions on enhanced cooperation, 'a clear preference emerged for not taking this issue on the IGC agenda'. At the Helsinki European Council, however, strong pressure was brought to bear by a number of member states, particularly Belgium, the Netherlands and Italy, which did not wish to foreclose the debate before the IGC had even begun. In the light of insistence that the conclusions be framed so as not to rule out any option at this early stage, a window was left open allowing the incoming Portuguese presidency to propose 'additional issues to be taken on the agenda'.

Because of these political sensitivities, the presidency had at all costs to avoid needlessly rigidifying positions at an early stage, which is always a risk in such ideologically driven debates. The Portuguese presidency did this in two ways. The first was by ensuring that the matter was handled in low-key, informal discussions among Representatives, without including it on agendas or producing formal papers. In such informal settings, Representatives were free to explore the broader implications off the record. The second was by prompting delegations to enter into a discussion about practical areas where enhanced co-operation might prove useful or desirable, before considering suitable legal means of achieving it. Areas mentioned on various occasions, although without tangible proposals being made, included security and defence, police and judicial cooperation, industry, research, and the environment. The presidency's overriding concern was to try and shed some of the dogmatism surrounding the debate and consider the practical uses to which such cooperation could be put. In the light of these discussions, it became clear that, provided certain equilibria were respected (see below), enhanced cooperation merited consideration with the prospect of enlargement, despite certain misgivings about the real need for treaty change. In its report to the Feira European Council, the presidency accordingly proposed its formal inclusion on the Conference's agenda. The Feira European Council in June endorsed this suggestion, confirming that 'the provisions on closer cooperation introduced into the Treaty of Amsterdam should also form part of the IGC's work, while respecting the need for coherence and solidarity in an enlarged Union'.

Content of the Negotiation

To date, apart from some flexibility in the scope of application of certain directives, enhanced cooperation in the treaty in any meaningful form has only actually been realized in clearly defined areas where all the relevant principles, rules and procedures governing that cooperation have been spelled out in the treaty or in treaty protocols. These types of arrangements, best exemplified by EMU and Schengen matters, have worked because underlying them was a clear political objective in a particular policy area linked to the single market, backed up with the necessary ways and means to achieve it. An IGC offers an ideal opportunity to emulate this approach in other areas. However, this is only possible if the Conference is able to identify suitable areas at a sufficiently early stage in its work to be in a position to specify all the relevant groundrules in the new treaty. During the Nice IGC no developed or detailed proposals for extending pre-determined enhanced cooperation in the treaties were forthcoming, despite ample opportunity being afforded by the Portuguese and French presidencies for member states to come forward with suggestions.

The real difficulty in this negotiation was that despite the best efforts of both presidencies, it proved extremely difficult to bring discussion down from the abstract to the practical. No tangible proposals, either modest or ambitious, were forthcoming from delegations for new areas where 'pre-determined' enhanced cooperation might be envisaged. In the absence of definite suggestions for areas to be covered, the Conference inevitably focused on reworking the enabling clauses introduced in the Treaty of Amsterdam (i.e. point 2(b) in Box 7.1). The problem was that to date these clauses had never been used, arguably because the conditions had been so tightly drawn as to make their use all but impossible (Weatherill 1999). The Conference accordingly found itself in the somewhat surreal position of considering amendments to treaty provisions which had never been used, to deal with situations which could not be clearly identified and for no clearly defined objective. If ever there was a subject in the realms of virtual reality this was it! However, given that the Union rarely likes to embark on abstract or theoretical negotiations out of choice, there were a number of underlying political reasons to explain the Conference's approach. These are analysed below after a description of the main changes made in the Treaty of Nice in recasting the Amsterdam enabling clauses into an operational instrument.

Main Issues Addressed in the Treaty of Nice

In reviewing the enabling clause provisions, four main problem areas emerged: (1) their scope of coverage; (2) decision-making procedures and institutional aspects; (3) the general principles and conditions governing enhanced cooperation; and (4) the overall presentation of the provisions in the treaties. The commentary below only highlights the key political negotiating points rather than detailing every treaty amendment. The Treaty of Nice provisions on enhanced cooperation in all three pillars are set out in full in Appendix 3.

Scope of Coverage of the Enabling Clauses

Defining the coverage of the enabling clauses was an issue in the EC Treaty and for the second pillar (i.e. Common Foreign and Security Policy). As far as the third pillar is concerned (cooperation in police and criminal justice matters), the existing broad potential coverage was retained.

Under the EC treaty, while enhanced cooperation is necessarily ruled out in areas of exclusive Community competence such as the CAP or the CCP (since member states cannot cooperate in areas where practically no national room for manoeuvre exists), there was justified concern that relaxing the requirements for launching enhanced cooperation risked fragmenting some of the Union's hard-won achievements, particularly the internal market. Allowing enhanced cooperation on regulatory or normative matters associated with establishing or preserving the internal market or the Union's financial solidarity would unquestionably be harmful to the interests of the Union as a whole and of those member states not involved from the outset. The debate in the latter stages of the IGC focused inevitably on how to safeguard these core areas of Community business. Provided the internal market and economic and social cohesion policies (i.e. structural and cohesion funds) were explicitly ringfenced, there would be no objective reason not to ease the conditions for enhanced cooperation in areas where member states in any case already had a significant measure of autonomy to act, without damaging the Union's coherence nor the interests of other member states. Suggestions were put forward for using enabling clauses for policy coordination within the limits of the margins for action left to member states in areas such as certain specifically targeted environmental protection measures and measures for securing the Union's external borders. Pushed in particular by Spain, the UK and others, the rationale of ringfencing broadly-defined core policies was agreed by the Conference without much difficulty. The treaty accordingly permits enhanced cooperation provided it 'does not concern areas which fall within the exclusive competence of the Community' (as in the Treaty of Amsterdam) and 'does not undermine the internal market as defined in article 14(2) of the TEC, or the economic and social cohesion established in accordance with Title XVII of that treaty' (Article 43 (d) and (e) TEU).

Enhanced cooperation under the second pillar (CFSP) has always been generally viewed with scepticism. Attempts to introduce such enabling clauses at Amsterdam failed. The value and strength of a common foreign policy is its unity and, on the face of it, using enabling clauses which would allow separate initiatives seems incompatible with the desired objective. Moreover, the treaty already contains provisions which allow a measure of flexibility. Article 23(1) TEU allows an 'opt out' for any member states which do not wish to apply a particular policy decision. It has been argued that constructive abstention in this way, which allows a number of member states not to apply a measure while accepting that it commits the Union, already provides sufficient flexibility without undermining the unity of the CFSP. While ways have been sought in the past to bind in all member states to the CFSP, particularly in the light of previous experience with contact groups, enhanced cooperation enabling clauses could never become a means of constraining member states' autonomy on the international scene. Spain, however, argued the need for an enabling clause to ensure that the development and application of CFSP actions by member states are clearly perceived as action by the Union rather than certain member states acting in isolation (IGC 2000d). The inclusion of a second pillar enabling clause in the treaty as part of the overhaul of the enhanced cooperation provisions was one of the more disputed aspects of discussion in the run-up to and at Nice itself. While the Conference originally considered texts which were broad in scope, including security and defence matters, the final outcome (see Appendix 3.3) is much more restricted in two respects:

- The main question was whether enhanced cooperation should be permissible only within an already agreed policy framework, or whether it should be conceived where there is no specific manifestation of the Union's policy in the form of a strategy, joint action or common position. The final scope agreed in the treaty is limited to the implementation of a joint action or a common position. In other words, it cannot relate to implementation of a common strategy, nor can it relate to matters which are not covered by joint actions or common positions. The scope is therefore extremely narrow.
- Matters having military or defence implications are excluded. The reason for this limited scope, as argued forcefully in particular by Sweden, Ireland and the UK, with the latter under intense media pressure about claims that the ESDP was the precursor of a European army, was that the new crisis management capabilities agreed at Nice, which the Union has invested so much time and effort in putting in place as a collective enterprise, should not be jeopardized by allowing enhanced cooperation initiatives. Accordingly references to security and defence, including initiatives in the field of armaments, were removed from the treaty at Nice.

From what has been outlined, enhanced cooperation on CFSP matters is evidently very different in nature from enhanced cooperation under the first and third pillars. In reality it is akin to a form of implementing measure of an already agreed policy accepted in principle by all member states under which specific tasks are delegated to the member states involved in enhanced cooperation. The term 'enhanced cooperation' is therefore something of a misnomer.

Decision-making Procedures

Easing some of the procedural requirements to make enhanced cooperation easier to initiate would depend on striking a balance between member states participating in enhanced cooperation and those electing not to participate at the outset. While this was also a concern at Amsterdam, at Nice adjustments were made in order to define more clearly the respective rights and obligations of 'ins' and 'outs' in any enhanced cooperation, thereby safeguarding the interests of both. In Amsterdam, member states had erred on the side of caution in introducing what were at that time innovatory provisions in the treaties. Despite the reluctance of certain member states to include enhanced cooperation on the IGC's agenda at the outset (most notably Sweden, Denmark, the UK and Ireland), it became clear particularly after Biarritz that an essential prerequisite for making progress would be to find the correct balance between making enhanced cooperation easier to launch in a particular area for those who wished to pursue it, and securing the interests of non participating member states, both in terms of safeguarding the Union *acquis* and of ensuring that they would not be arbitrarily excluded from taking part if they elected to do so and fulfilled the relevant criteria laid down in the treaties. As far as the procedures for launching enhanced cooperation are concerned, these can be summarized as follows:

• The first is that the *minimum number of member states* required to launch any initiative will in future be reduced from a majority of member states to eight. During the Conference various options were explored, some of which involved differentiating the procedure for launching enhanced cooperation on the basis of the number of member states involved; the fewer the number of member states, the more rigorous the procedure. Early on, a consensus emerged around a baseline figure of around one-third of member states in EU-27 as a minimum critical mass. The Conference finally agreed to the absolute figure of eight rather than one-third, which avoids any reduction in the figure for EU-15, but reduces the minimum percentage of member states required as the Union enlarges.

- Second, the *ability of a member state to veto* any enhanced cooperation initiative in the first and third pillars has been removed. In future, qualified majority will be the rule, although a member of the Council may delay a decision by requesting that the matter be referred to the European Council. Since the European Council in practice meets every three months, this does not represent a significant delay. This referral does not constitute a veto, since the matter will revert to the Council after it has been discussed by the European Council.

- As far as *enhanced cooperation under the second pillar* is concerned, the procedure used for establishing enhanced cooperation is identical to the normal CFSP procedure, which involves QMV coupled with the possibility for one member state to apply the 'emergency brake' veto. This provision, which at Amsterdam was applicable for initiating enhanced cooperation under the first and third pillars, was widely considered to be one of the factors which rendered the existing provisions unworkable. While it has been abolished in the first and third pillars, it has been retained for second pillar enhanced cooperation, to ensure parallelism of decision-making procedures with mainstream CFSP decisions. This raises some doubt about whether these provisions will ever be used. The procedure allowing other member states to join is analogous to that found in the current third pillar.

Four other institutional features are worth noting. The first concerns the role and place of the Commission in the procedure for launching enhanced cooperation. Many, including the Commission itself, felt that the Commission's position should be strengthened, particularly under second and third pillars by, for example, requiring unanimity in the Council to launch enhanced cooperation in the event of the Commission issuing a negative opinion, and using the procedure foreseen in the TEC for member states to join enhanced cooperation under the third pillar. While these suggestions failed to rally majority support, under the second pillar the Commission must give its opinion particularly on whether the enhanced cooperation proposed is consistent with Union policies. Second, the European Parliament's role has not been substantially altered, other than to correct the anomaly of not giving the Parliament an appropriate say on initiating enhanced cooperation under the

TEC in areas where codecision applies. Article 11(2) TEC accordingly foresees that the European Parliament must give its assent if enhanced cooperation is envisaged in any such areas. Third, once enhanced cooperation has been launched, the population clause foreseen in Article 205 will not apply to decisions to be taken by QMV in that framework of the enhanced cooperation. Fourth, the Secretary-General/High Representative has been accorded a specific role in keeping all members of the Council and the European Parliament fully informed of implementation of enhanced cooperation under the CFSP.

General Principles and Conditions
The general principles and conditions governing enhanced cooperation have been clarified in two ways. First of all, certain changes have been made to language which if interpreted in a strictly legal sense would make initiation of enhanced cooperation virtually impossible. Second, as a counterpart to relaxing the decision-making procedures for initiating enhanced cooperation, the interests of non-participating member states have been safeguarded by basing decisions for them to join any existing enhanced cooperation as far as possible on objective rather than politically subjective criteria.

In addition to making enhanced cooperation easier to launch, the Treaty of Nice has removed a number of conditions laid down in the Amsterdam Treaty text which could potentially be invoked as a means of blocking any meaningful cooperation. For example, the reference to enhanced cooperation 'not discriminating among member states' has been removed since any enhanced cooperation, by virtue of the fact that it differentiates between member states, could be construed as discriminatory. Similarly, the reference to enhanced cooperation not affecting the 'interests' of non-participating states have also been removed, precisely because it is a purely subjective criteria which could be invoked by any member state seeking to block any enhanced cooperation initiative. The treaty does, however, retain the objective conditions that enhanced cooperation must respect the 'competences, rights and obligations' of non-participating member states.

Two kinds of amendments have been introduced to reflect concerns about the risk of member states being excluded from enhanced cooperation on purely political grounds. First, a number of general petitions of principle have been included going in the direction of encouraging maximum inclusiveness of any measure by stressing that enhanced cooperation in the Union must be aimed at 'protecting and serving its interests and at reinforcing the process of integration' (Article 43(a)). The Commission and the member states participating in enhanced cooperation shall also ensure that as many member states as possible are encouraged to take part. The Council and the Commission must ensure the consistency of activities undertaken on the basis of the enhanced cooperation enabling clauses and the consistency of such activities with the policies of the Union and the Community. While the concept of last resort already existed in the Treaty of Amsterdam 'where the objective of the said treaties could not be attained by applying the relevant procedures', Article 43a allows enhanced cooperation in future only as a last resort 'when it has been established within the Council that the objectives of such cooperation cannot be attained within a reasonable period by applying the relevant provisions of the Treaties'; this implies that a clear cut-off point must somehow be reached in the Council before enhanced cooperation can be initiated. The Treaty leaves open the way in which any such cut-off point will be determined. Second, Article 43(j) enshrines the principle of openness. Article 43b gives tangible effect to this by emphasizing that enhanced cooperation is 'open to all Member states at any time...subject to compliance with the basic decision and with the decisions taken in that framework'. The treaty has attempted to ensure as far as possible that any decision to allow non participating member states to join is not a matter of political opportunism, but based purely on an assessment as to whether they fulfil a number of objective criteria.

Presentation of Enhanced Cooperation in the Treaties
Overall presentation was an issue for two reasons. First, all participants agreed on the need for the provisions to be simplified and presented in a more rational form by grouping together all the general principles and conditions in the TEU, thereby simplifying in each of the relevant treaty titles the operational provisions for launching enhanced cooperation and allowing non-participants to join at a later date. While lawyers may be critical of the fact that a number of the general conditions laid down in Article 40 are repetitive or redundant from a strictly legal point of view, sometimes repetition provides the necessary reassurance for obtaining agreement, bearing in mind that negotiating a treaty is as much a political as a legal drafting exercise. Second, given that discussion had been informally initiated in the Conference on a pragmatic

basis without focusing initially on the different pillars, calls were made to group all the enhanced cooperation provisions in a single title in the TEU to enhance the political presentation of the outcome. This latter idea did not rally significant support and, although possible, inserting placeholders in the TEC and the appropriate titles of the TEU would have involved certain legal complications.

Nice Enabling Clauses: Legal Fine-tuning or Political Necessity?

The Treaty of Nice has done much more than simply legally fine-tuning the enhanced cooperation enabling clauses. Despite initial reticence, this final result was a substantial reworking of the clauses which were achieved without major political hiccups. They have become at least a potentially usable instrument. Given the edginess which prevailed at the start of the Conference, such an outcome may appear remarkable. However, three political factors may help to explain this.

First, while enabling clauses were arguably unlikely to be used in the Union of 15 quite simply because they were not needed, the prospect of expansion from 15 to 27 members raised real fears about the Union being transformed from a known to an unknown quantity. With enlargement looming ever nearer, and involving states with levels of prosperity well below that of existing members, the view was widely shared that in a larger and more heterogeneous Union, it might be wise to take out an insurance policy for the future in the shape of workable enhanced cooperation enabling clauses. Even if no clearly perceived purpose exists for these clauses at present, in part because of the difficulty for member states to work in a mindset of EU-27, the more instruments at the disposal of the Union the better equipped it will be to deal with unforeseen eventualities. Even if ideas on precisely how these clauses might be used in the context of enlargement were sketchy, there was no suggestion that recourse to enhanced cooperation enabling clauses would result in a *de facto* 'core' Europe, which was a concern reflected in many of the position papers submitted to the Conference by candidate states.

Second, enabling clauses which were easier to use could act as a deterrent to states seeking solutions or constituting a 'core' group outside the Union's institutional framework. Like any effective deterrent, the possibility of using the provisions must be credible, even if they are never actually used. Interestingly, there did not appear to be any real concern that easing the conditions might lead to them being turned into a means for across-the-board, systematic cooperation by a group of member states seeking to establish an integrationist 'vanguard' within the Union. The general view was that the enabling clauses should be an instrument of last resort to be used on a case-by-case basis by discrete groups of member states on specific issues when circumstances genuinely warranted their use. Even the joint German/Italian initiative on closer cooperation, while arguing for enhanced cooperation to allow a number of member states to take a lead on integration by forming 'an open, functional avant-garde which will serve the process of integration', did not envisage systematic use of enabling clauses for creating a pioneer group. In their view 'the instrument of enhanced cooperation must under all circumstances be used in a selective and politically responsible manner' (IGC 2000g).

Third, including enhanced cooperation into the Conference offered the possibility of widening the scope of the package within which trade-offs could be transacted in finding an overall political balance in an otherwise limited and difficult negotiating agenda.

Much of the ideological rhetoric which was a feature of discussions at Amsterdam had given way to a more pragmatic view of the exercise, with both enthusiasts and sceptics willing to examine ways of seeking a genuine balance between the interests of participating member states and those who might choose to remain outside in the first instance. The revised treaty provisions have undoubtedly gone a long way in the direction of removing artificial political barriers standing in the way of initiatives that would have little impact on the interests of non-participating member states. The fact that most of these substantive provisions were largely agreed in advance of Nice suggests that the Conference has succeeded in this balancing act, at least sufficiently to satisfy the needs of political presentation in all member states.

As regards the negotiating process, representatives and ministers invested the necessary time and effort in considering the ramifications and addressing the political difficulties raised (Stubb 2001). Ministers discussed the more political aspects of enhanced cooperation, particularly in the second pillar, on no less than five occasions. As a result, by the time these matters were submitted to heads of government a predictable and manageable number of points were actually raised in Biarritz and Nice. This confirms the view that an IGC works best where preparation is effectively carried out and subjects presented to heads of government have already been properly processed at political level.

The Union will, in all likelihood, go cautiously in having recourse to these new instruments; the first occasion they are used will constitute an important precedent. Irrespective of the way in which they might be used in future, these reworked provisions have probably weakened the case for structured vanguard groups of member states organizing themselves outside the treaties. It is one thing for a number of member states to agree among themselves to act as a unit and coordinate their positions as far as possible inside the EU institutions, using all the means available under the treaties to promote the interests of the group. At the end of the day, if certain member states wish to take a political initiative to work within the system according to their own code of behaviour as a sort of internal pressure group, they cannot be prevented from doing so. It is, however, quite another to conclude a treaty in parallel to the existing Union; how could such a separate treaty strengthen rather than weaken the existing Union? Creating new structures, such as the 'light secretariat' hinted at by President Chirac in his Bundestag speech, runs a serious risk of further undermining public understanding of and support for the European enterprise as a whole. If the enhanced cooperation provisions in the Treaty of Nice have succeeded in laying such ideas to rest, that alone will have justified the negotiating effort expended on them.

8 |

Other Institutions, Bodies and Issues

The Helsinki European Council called on the IGC to examine 'other necessary amendments to the Treaties arising as regards the European institutions...and in implementing the Treaty of Amsterdam'. This chapter looks at the reforms agreed relating to the institutions and bodies not covered in previous chapters, in particular the key changes which have been introduced into the Treaty of Nice concerning the Court of Justice and the Court of First Instance (CFI). Amendments have also been made regarding the Court of Auditors, the Economic and Social Committee and the Committee of the Regions. This chapter also describes succinctly the other points contained in the Treaty of Nice which cover an eclectic range of questions not directly related to enlargement, but which can be broadly construed as 'other necessary amendments arising...in implementing the Treaty of Amsterdam'. The common thread linking all the issues described in this chapter, with the exception of amendments to Article 7 TEU on fundamental rights, is that they did not detain Representatives or ministers for any substantial length of time, either because they proved on the whole to be relatively uncontroversial or, in the case of the Court of Justice, because the detailed preparatory work was efficiently carried out by the Friends of the Presidency Group working to a mandate from Representatives.

The Court of Justice and the Court of First Instance

The Court of Justice is entrusted with ensuring that the law is observed in interpreting and applying the treaty. While it generally has a low public profile compared to the Union's policy-making institutions (except when delivering judgments such as the Bosman ruling which radically transformed the football transfer system), it is an essential component of the Union's unique institutional architecture and has played a fundamental role in the Union's development since its inception, including the establishment of the *de facto* primacy of Community law over conflicting national legislation (see Shaw 2000). It ensures that EU institutions and member states act lawfully and that national courts know how to apply EU law. As a result of the growing caseload, a Court of First Instance was attached to the Court of Justice in 1988.

The problem being faced by the Courts is quite simply one of judicial overload. The number of new cases is increasing at a faster rate than cases are being cleared, and the time it takes for the Courts to deal with cases is becoming longer. At the end of 1999, 1628 cases were pending before the Court of Justice and the Court of First Instance, compared with 608 pending cases in 1988, and the average time for a preliminary ruling rose from 17 months in 1988 to 23 months in 1999 making it increasingly cumbersome for national courts to seek assistance on matters of EU law. The reasons for this mushrooming caseload are threefold. The increase in litigation in the Union mirrors a general trend found in all member states in the latter half of the twentieth century as citizens in an ever more sophisticated society appear much more willing and able to seek judicial remedies to defend their rights. Two further factors are particular to the Union's judicial bodies: one is the impact of successive enlargements and the resultant increase in caseload as the Union expands geographically in size. The second is the increase in the scope and quantity of the EU's legislative activity following the Treaties of Maastricht and Amsterdam which granted the Court additional jurisdiction in economic and monetary union and in asylum and immigration, as well as in the work of the EU trademarks office in Alicante. The Courts' predicament was examined in depth by independent experts (Due 2000), the Court itself (ECJ 2000) and the Commission (Commission 2000b). The need for reform of the system to relieve the strains to which it is already subject and ensure uniformity of application and consistency of EU law after enlargement was uncontested by any member state.

The main question of method was whether structural changes in the judicial system required to cope with enlargement should already be addressed in substance in the treaty, or whether the Conference's work should be confined to introducing enabling clauses in the treaty to allow the Union to adjust provisions on the Court to new circumstances in future without the need to resort to a cumbersome IGC procedure. While delegations initially tended to support one or other of these basic positions, it became clear early on that a balance would probably have to be found combining both approaches in view of the limited time at the Conference's disposal. This involved a substantial rewriting of Articles 220 to 229a and Article 245, as well as a complete reorganization of the Statute of the Court of Justice. In balancing both approaches, the treaties have undertaken a minimal number of reforms which will enter into force immediately. Coping adequately with the challenge of enlargement will require exploiting to the full the opportunities opened up in the Treaty and the Statute which are described below.

Four categories of issue relating to the Courts were examined by the Conference: first, the inevitable questions of size and composition; second, issues relating to internal organization and structure; third, the allocation of jurisdiction between the Court of Justice and the Court of First Instance as well as the possible setting up of new entities to deal with specialized areas of litigation; and fourth, whether to apply a more rational arrangement of the various provisions relating to the Court of Justice and the Court of First Instance as they appear in the Treaty, the Statute and their respective rules of procedure.

Given the fact that a considerable amount of detailed technical reworking of the provisions relating to the Court of Justice and the Court of First Instance would be required, the Conference decided that this would be best handled by legal experts. A Friends of the Presidency Group, consisting of Legal Counsellors from Permanent Representations and capitals, as well as Commission representatives and European Parliament observers, was accordingly mandated to examine the division of competences between jurisdictions, how to deal with different categories of action, the rules of procedure and the composition of the Courts. The Group met throughout the Portuguese and French presidencies. Regular progress reports were submitted to the Representatives Group, which also highlighted sticking points on which a steer was required from Representatives or ministers to guide further work. Representatives and the Friends Group also held an informal meeting with the presidents of the Court of Justice and the Court of First Instance.

Size and Composition of the Courts
The principal question was whether the Court should continue to have one judge from each member state or whether the number should be limited given that the Court frequently sits in plenary session. The Court itself took no stance in favour of one option or the other given the

politically sensitive nature of the question. The issue was not dissimilar to that regarding the Commission: whether the collegiate nature of the Court would be best preserved by limiting the number of judges or by enshrining the principle of one judge from each member state and making appropriate adjustments in the Court's internal structure. However, the issue of size was much less politicized than in the case of the Commission, and the principle of one judge from each member state was accepted practically at the outset by a large majority of delegations. Given that the Court of Justice is responsible for ensuring the uniform application of Community law and that it is applied first and foremost through national courts, the argument of having each national legal tradition and system represented by a judge thoroughly familiar with that tradition proved to be telling. Article 221 accordingly states that 'the Court of Justice shall consist of one Judge from each Member state'. This wording deliberately avoided the term 'national', since it theoretically allows the possibility of a member state appointing a judge of a different nationality than the nationality of the appointing state. Some delegations were unhappy at previous formulations of this principle which indicated that the Court of Justice would consist of a number of judges equal to the number of member states, since they feared that worded in this way, the treaty could allow the possibility of, say, two French judges and no German judge! A similar provision exists for the Court of First Instance, which shall consist of 'at least one Judge from each Member state', with the number of judges to be determined in the Statute of the Court of Justice (Article 224). The treaty did not change the number of Advocates-General (eight); given the impact of enlargement, the possibility has been retained of increasing their number should the Court itself request it (Article 223). No changes were made in judges' mandates (six years renewable).

Internal Structure of the Courts
The treaty enshrines the principle of the Court sitting in chambers (of three or five judges), a Grand Chamber and plenary session. The main innovation is the creation of the Grand Chamber of eleven judges, presided over by the president of the Court and including the presidents of the five judge Chambers as well as other judges (Article 221 and Article 16 of the Statute). The fact that presidents of five judge chambers are to be elected for three years and that they will automatically sit in the Grand Chamber encountered initial resistance from a

number of member states which considered that these provisions were contrary to the principle of equality of judges and could lead to operational problems on account of the accumulated workload of the persons in question. Many considered, however, that this was necessary in the interests of efficiency of a larger Court of Justice, although as a compromise, this provision was included in the Statute rather than in the treaty itself. The Grand Chamber will sit when a member state or a Community institution that is party to the proceedings so requests. For certain cases listed in the Statute as well as cases of exceptional importance, the Court will sit in plenary session. Article 50 of the Statute provides for the Court of First Instance to sit in chambers of three or five judges, although in certain cases (governed by the rules of procedure) the Court may sit in plenary session or be constituted by a single judge.

Jurisdiction of the Courts

The Commission suggested in its supplementary contribution to the Conference on the Court (European Commission 2000b) that the treaty should undertake a new allocation of competences between the Court of Justice and the Court of First Instance in order to give general responsibility for dealing with actions to the Court of First Instance, thereby limiting the intervention of the Court itself to matters essential for the Community's legal order as the Union's supreme legal body. Under the Treaty of Nice, a three-tier structure of judicial bodies has been created (see Box 8.1), under which the Court of First Instance is given much wider general responsibilities for hearing a variety of classes of action.

One of the main reasons for the Court being overburdened was the ever-increasing volume of references for a preliminary ruling under Article 234. Many considered that the interaction between the Court and national courts through this procedure had contributed to the former's success and that the Conference should be cautious about changing it. The treaty has, however, given the Court of First Instance jurisdiction to hear and determine questions referred for a preliminary ruling under Article 234 in certain specific areas to be determined in the Statute at a later date (probably in areas where the CFI has first instance or appellate jurisdiction).

Box 8.1: The Union's new judicial structure

Court of Justice

One Judge from each member state plus eight Advocates-General

Competent for all matters not under the jurisdiction of the
Court of First Instance or judicial panels,
in particular preliminary rulings under Article 234
(except preliminary rulings for which the CFI has jurisdiction)

Appeal of decisions by the Court of First Instance on points of law only

Decisions by the CFI on actions against decisions
by judicial panels and on preliminary rulings
may also exceptionally be subject to review

Court of First Instance

At least one Judge from each member state

Jurisdiction to hear matters under:
—Article 230 (Legality of acts)
—Article 232 (Failure to act)
—Article 234 (Preliminary rulings only in certain specific areas)
—Article 235 (Compensation for damage)
—Article 236 (Staff disputes)
—Article 238 (Arbitration)
other than matters assigned to judicial panels and those reserved
in the Statute of the Court of Justice (cf. Article 51)

Jurisdiction to hear actions brought against decisions of judicial panels

The CFI may refer cases on decisions in principle likely to affect
the unity and consistency of Community law to the ECJ

Judicial Panels

To be created by the Council for certain classes of action in specific areas

---

Suggestions had been made, including by the Court itself, to create in the treaty a number of specialized panels to deal in particular with staff cases and cases relating to trademarks, given the specialized nature of both. Certain member states were reluctant to create such specialized judicial panels already in the treaty. A compromise was found by introducing an enabling clause in Article 225a allowing the Council to create judicial panels to hear and determine at first instance certain classes of action or proceeding brought in specific areas. Decisions by judicial panels may be subject to a right of appeal to the Court of First Instance on points of law or when provided for in the decision, on points of fact. A declaration included in the final act calls on the Court of Justice and the Commission to prepare a draft decision establishing a judicial panel for delivering judgments in EU staff cases as soon as possible. With regard to trademarks, a new Article 229a allows the Council to adopt provisions to confer jurisdiction on the Court of Justice in disputes relating to the application of acts adopted on the basis of the treaty which creates Community industrial property rights. Any such provisions will require adoption by member states in accordance with their respective constitutional requirements. The Conference noted that Article 229a does not prejudge the choice of the judicial framework which may be set up to deal with disputes relating to the application of acts which create Community industrial property rights. Luxembourg undertook in a formal declaration not to claim the seat of Boards of Appeal of the Office for Harmonization in the Internal Market (trade marks and designs) which will remain in Alicante, even if these Boards were to become judicial panels.

Restructuring and Rationalization of Provisions Relating to the Courts
Provisions regarding the constitution and functioning of the Courts are currently found in the main body of the treaty, in the three Statutes on the Court of Justice (for the EC, ECSC and Euratom) only part of which (Title III) could be amended by the Council, the rules of procedure of both Courts (which required unanimous approval by the Council) and in the 1988 Council decision establishing the Court of First Instance. These texts have now been substantially reorganized and repackaged in a more rational form. A number of detailed provisions contained in the treaty were moved to the Statute, into which the three existing EC, ECSC and Euratom Statutes were incorporated. The new Statute in the Treaty of Nice has also incorporated the substantive

content of the decision establishing the Court of First Instance. Moreover, Article 245 has given the Council the power to amend all provisions of the Statute except Title I which relates to the status, obligations and rights of judges and Advocates-General. Moreover, by placing in the Statute politically sensitive provisions formerly contained in the rules of procedure, such as rules governing the use of languages in the Courts, qualified majority voting in the Council was accepted for approving the rules of procedure drawn up by the Court of Justice and the Court of First Instance (as well as judicial panels in future). These changes represent a significant and necessary reform and have undoubtedly introduced greater clarity and flexibility into the system.

Other Issues Relating to the Courts
The Conference also examined a number of other suggestions to amend the treaties on points not directly linked to the objective of improving the efficiency of the Court of Justice in preparation for enlargement. Two of these related in particular to the European Parliament's role under Articles 230 and 300(6), and have been examined in Chapter 6. The third concerned Article 68 relating to the Court's powers under Title IV of the EC Treaty on visas, asylum, immigration and judicial cooperation in civil matters. Under Article 68, only national courts of last resort have the right and obligation to refer questions to the Court of Justice. This provision was inserted in the Treaty of Amsterdam when these matters were placed within the scope of the EC Treaty because of fears that the Court might be overwhelmed, in particular by asylum cases. A number of delegations considered that the treaty should either revert to the normal judicial arrangements for preliminary rulings or allow for an accelerated procedure in asylum and immigration cases. However, neither of these suggestions rallied substantial support.

Court of Auditors

The Court of Auditors is the institution with responsibility for looking into the legality and regularity of revenue and expenditure and the soundness of financial management in the Union. Although the treaty did not stipulate that the Court of Auditors must be made up of a national of each member state, that was always the case in practice. The main question relating to the Court's size was whether to continue to allow the Court to grow with each new accession to the Union or whether to cap the membership at the present level or lower, as the Commission had suggested. The Commission considered that the institution's effectiveness would be preserved by limiting the number of members to twelve, arguing that increases in the Community budget did not lead to a corresponding increase in the need for audits or reports. While this view, which was supported by a number of member states, emphasized the fact that the Court of Auditors is not an intergovernmental body, the Treaty of Nice maintained the current practice by requiring the Court of Auditors to be composed of one member from each member state. There were two reasons why this view prevailed: the first was the fact that a significant number of delegations considered that having a member from each member state would facilitate cooperation with national audit bodies, a view shared by the Court of Auditors itself (Court of Auditors 2000a). However, perhaps more telling was a tactical desire on the part of the presidency not to push too hard on limiting the size of the Court of Auditors in order to deploy maximum political effort on limiting the size of the Commission.

Members will be appointed by the Council acting by qualified majority on the basis of a list drawn up in accordance with the proposals made by each member state. As in the case of the appointment of members of the Economic and Social Committee and the Committee of the Regions, this is in reality a 'false' qualified majority because in all three cases, the Council will simply endorse candidates put forward by each member state. While the practical effects of QMV may be minimal, it constitutes (along with the more significant introduction of QMV for the appointment of the president of the Commission and Secretary-General of the Council/High Representative for the CFSP) a breach in the unanimity rule for appointments in the Union which paves the way for all appointments to be made by QMV in future.

As far as the internal structure of the Court of Auditors is concerned, given the fact that their number will increase in future, the treaty expressly allowed the Court to establish internal chambers in order to adopt certain categories of report or opinions under the conditions laid down by its rules of procedure. The latter will in future be approved by the Council by qualified majority. As part of the effort to improve the protection of the Community's financial interests, a declaration attached to the final act expressly allows the president of the Court of Auditors to set up a contact committee with the chairmen of national audit institutions in order to improve cooperation between them.

Economic and Social Committee and the Committee of the Regions

The main question relating to these two consultative assemblies was at what level the size of both bodies should be capped and whether to maintain parity of size. The Treaty of Nice has retained parity and extrapolated the current membership for existing member states to EU-27 (see Appendix 1). From the outset, there was considerable pressure to undertake a straightforward extrapolation of the number of members from each member state in the Committee of the Regions as the best means of ensuring that the regional dimension in each member state was properly represented (particularly those with federal or devolved structures). Despite attempts to fix the size of the Economic and Social Committee at a lower level, intense lobbying by the Committee itself ensured that parity has been maintained. Both will grow to 344 members in EU-27 within an overall ceiling for each in the treaty of 350 members.

Important changes have been made in the composition of each body. Following calls that the Economic and Social Committee should be more representative of all sectors of civil society, the treaty has modified the composition of the Committee to include 'representatives of the various economic and social components of organised civil society, and in particular representatives of producers, farmers, carriers, workers, dealers, craftsmen, professional occupations, consumers and the general interest', thereby broadening the scope of interests represented while retaining the existing list of socio-economic categories in Article 257 (with the addition of a reference to consumers) in response to lobbying by various interest groups themselves. Membership of the Committee of the Regions will in future be linked to holding a regional or local authority electoral mandate or being politically accountable to an elected assembly, with membership of the Committee of the Regions automatically lapsing should the mandate come to an end. As previously mentioned, members of both bodies will be appointed by QMV.

Fundamental Rights

In parallel with the IGC, the Convention established by the Cologne European Council was engaged in drawing up the Charter of Fundamental Rights for the European Union which was solemnly proclaimed in Nice by the European Parliament, the Council and the Commission. The Convention completed its work in advance of the Biarritz informal European Council, at which it was agreed that the Charter would be proclaimed as a political document in Nice, without being given legal status by being incorporated into or alluded to in the treaty, given strong resistance in particular by Denmark, the UK and Ireland. The Charter was not therefore part of the Conference's work.

Two subjects relating to fundamental rights were discussed by the Conference. The first was the suggestion by Finland (IGC 2000e) to create a legal basis in the treaty to enable the European Community to accede to the European Convention on Human Rights. While all member states are parties to this Convention, no basis exists in the EC treaty for the Community as such to accede. However, this suggestion, which was considered in detail during the Amsterdam IGC and which raises complex legal issues regarding the relationship between the jurisdiction of the European Court of Human Rights and the Court of Justice (see, for example, Shaw 2000), failed to rally significant support.

The second related to action by the Union in the event of breach of the principles on which the Union is founded. Article 7 TEU allows the Union to take action in the event of a determination by the Council of a serious and persistent breach of these principles by a member state. This provision, which was introduced in the Treaty of Amsterdam, came under intense scrutiny in the Conference against the backdrop of the measures taken by fourteen member states bilaterally against Austria following the formation of a government including members of the Freedom Party. This prompted a wider debate on this issue with the prospect of enlargement. Some suggestions were made for amending the existing provisions contained in Article 7, but most delegations felt that the issue had been thoroughly discussed at Amsterdam and that Article 7, as a 'nuclear deterrent' provision containing exceptional measures to deal with exceptional circumstances, should not be tampered with. However, many delegations, in the light of proposals tabled by Belgium, Austria, the Commission and the Portuguese presidency, felt that an additional provision could be inserted into Article 7 to establish an early warning procedure for determining the existence in a member state of a *risk* of a serious breach of fundamental rights. Some scepticism prevailed initially on the principle of including such a provision in the treaty, since some delegations considered that it would be difficult or impossible to determine objectively the kind of circumstances in which it might be required, and that in the event of political action of this type being necessary, it might be preferable to handle it as a purely political measure, rather than subject to a rigid procedural and legal framework. The majority view, however, was that the current arrangements under Article 7 TEU should be supplemented in order to place any action by the Union within a structured framework of rules laid down in the treaty.

Box 8.2: New first paragraph to Article 7 TEU added in the Treaty of Nice

---

Article 7 TEU

1. On a reasoned proposal by one third of the Member States, by the European Parliament or by the Commission, the Council, acting by a majority of four-fifths of its members after obtaining the assent of the European Parliament, may determine that there is a clear risk of a serious breach by a Member State of the principles mentioned in Article 6(1), and address appropriate recommendations to that State. Before making such a determination, the Council shall hear the Member State in question and, acting in accordance with the same procedure, may call on independent persons to submit within a reasonable time period a report on the situation in the Member State in question.

The Council shall regularly verify that the grounds on which such a determination was made continue to apply.

With majority support for the idea in principle, the Conference had to address three questions: the content of the provision, the procedure to be used for implementing it and whether it would be subject to judicial review. As far as the content was concerned, given the range of views presented, a balance had to be struck in the new provision between the possibility for the Council to issue recommendations to member states where a clear risk of a serious breach of the Union's fundamental principles is found to exist, and the right for the member state concerned to have a fair hearing, as well as the obligation incumbent on the Council to verify regularly that the grounds for its determination continue to exist. This latter point was particularly important for Denmark, where the action taken by the Fourteen was deemed to have played a role in the outcome of the Danish referendum on the euro.

Two main political points remained until the end: the question of the procedure for making a determination, and the possibility of judicial review of any decision taken by the Council. On the first point, the

French presidency and a number of delegations favoured qualified majority voting. However, many felt that qualified majority voting was inappropriate for fundamental decisions of this type for which each member state's vote should count equally. Member states initially reluctant to contemplate inclusion of such a provision, argued that in any case a more stringent voting procedure should be used, without resorting to unanimity. A compromise was found on the basis of four-fifths of the members of the Council originally proposed by the Portuguese presidency. This reinforced majority means that in a Union of up to 20 member states, a determination requires unanimity less two (including the member state concerned) and in a Union comprising 21 member states or more, unanimity less three (including the member state concerned). As far as judicial review was concerned, acceptance of this new provision in Nice by Austria was conditional on including an amendment in Article 46 TEU which extended the jurisdiction of the Court of Justice to cover 'the purely procedural stipulations in Article 7, with the Court of Justice acting at the request of the Member State concerned within one month from the date of the determination by the Council provided for in that Article.'

Security and Defence

Completing the process launched at Cologne in June 1999, the Nice European Council took a number of decisions to put in place the definitive structures necessary for the Union to assume its responsibilities in military and civilian crisis management operations as part of the Common European Policy on Security and Defence. Although the reports for the European Council were prepared in different fora as an entirely separate exercise, the key question as far as the IGC was concerned was whether any treaty revision would be required in putting in place the new structures. Since this could only be assessed properly at the end of the process, the IGC did not embark on any substantive discussion before Nice except on the question of whether to allow enhanced cooperation on security and defence matters under the second pillar (see Chapter 7). The Benelux States and Italy submitted a joint paper to the Conference in October calling for a number of changes in Article 17 TEU relating to the Western European Union (WEU), and Article 25 TEU on the role of the Political and Security Committee (IGC 2000h). At the time, however, most delegations took the view that treaty revision would probably not be strictly necessary and it was considered premature at that juncture to enter into detailed discussion. This question was held open until Nice itself.

Pushed in particular by the Dutch delegation, amendments to Articles 17 and 25 TEU were again tabled and accepted by heads of government. A declaration to the final act accompanying the changes makes clear that the objective for the Union is to become operational quickly and that the ratification of the treaty changes does not constitute a precondition for the necessary operational decisions being taken on the basis of the existing treaty provisions. These amendments involved:

- removing from Article 17 TEU various references to the WEU, other than the reference contained in paragraph 4 which relates to the WEU and NATO collective defence commitment. This reflects the reality that the WEU has for all practical purposes withered away with the exception of its Article V collective defence commitment. These changes represent essentially a tidying up exercise to bring the treaty into line with the new security and defence reality within the Union. The WEU's tasks have been subsumed by the Union, where the definitive military and politico-military structures have now been put in place, supported by the Union's military staff in the Council Secretariat. Moreover, the post of Secretary-General of the WEU has been double hatted with Secretary-General of the Council in the person of Javier Solana.

- and, more importantly, giving the Political and Security Committee, whose members are usually based in Permanent Representations in Brussels, though it also meets regularly at Political Director level, responsibility not only for monitoring day-to-day foreign and security policy business in the Council, but exercising political control and strategic direction of crisis management operations. Article 25 TEU also expressly allows the Council to authorize the Committee for the duration of crisis management operations to take the relevant decisions concerning the political control and strategic direction of the operation. Given the reluctance with which some member states viewed the prospect of treaty change in this area, this proposal passed remarkably easily. It means that as in organizations such as NATO, operational decisions in times of crisis can be devolved from ministerial to civil servant level, under the political responsibility of the Council.

These changes underscore just how far the Union has come in security and defence in recent years. Four years ago in Amsterdam these changes would have been inconceivable.

EMU Issues

Aside from the extension of QMV for certain EMU provisions and the question of whether or not to abolish the cooperation procedure for adopting legislation which only applies for certain EMU matters (see Chapter 6), two other treaty changes were made in the EMU chapter. These are described below. What was particularly noteworthy about these changes was the procedure whereby they were prepared. For IGCs, as for any major package negotiation in the Union, steps are taken to ensure that the negotiation is handled in a single preparatory framework for two main reasons: first, it ensures internal coherence in the negotiation and that a single forum has a clear overview of the key political issues; second, it avoids the risk of fragmentation into different vested departmental interests which would undermine the chances of achieving a coherent and substantial outcome. This did not, however, stop the Economic and Financial Committee (EFC) and the ECOFIN Council considering on an informal basis a number of issues relating to their particular policy field. Such informal discussions were kept low key (e.g. at ECOFIN ministers' lunches) and ministers' views were reflected in the form of a letter from the president of the ECOFIN Council to the president of the IGC ministerial sessions. This work nevertheless yielded a further extension of qualified majority voting for Articles 111(4) and 123(4). More significantly, this is yet another illustration of the authority and influence of Finance ministers within the Council and the effectiveness with which this sector tends to operate, in making a generally positive contribution to the Conference's overall outcome. For these changes the opinion of the European Central Bank (ECB) had to be sought in accordance with Article 48 of the TEU (see Chapter 2).

Operation of the ECB Governing Council

A new paragraph 10.6 has been added in Article 10 of the Statute of the European Central Bank to allow the Council (meeting in the composition of heads of state or government) to amend paragraph 2 of the same article relating to the working methods of the ECB's Governing Council. This amendment relates principally to the question of voting rights in the Governing Council. The question as to whether a Governing Council of 27 members could function effectively had been raised before Nice, but no proposal was actually tabled. Any future decisions will be subject to national ratification. The expectation is for a recommendation to be presented as soon as possible in order to enable the Governing Council to adapt its decision-making procedures to the requirements of enlargement.

Amendment of the Statute of the European Investment Bank
The statute of the EIB is laid down in a protocol to the treaty. Amending Article 266 EC to allow the Council to amend Articles 4 (subscriptions to the Bank's capital), 11 (composition of the Board of Directors), 12 (voting procedure for the Board of Directors) and 18(5) (ratio of outstanding guarantees to the Bank's capital) was considered necessary in order to introduce a sufficient degree of flexibility to cope with enlargement.

Venue for European Councils

As part of the process of reaching an overall agreement in Nice, the Conference agreed to include in the final act the following declaration which fixes the venue of the European Council in Brussels: 'As from 2002, one European Council meeting per presidency will be held in Brussels. When the Union comprises eighteen members, all European Council meetings will be held in Brussels'. Feelings about this declaration have been mixed. Some have emphasized that, in addition to cost savings, basing European Councils in Brussels undoubtedly represents a further step towards institutionalizing the Union's supreme political authority. With the trend towards holding at least four meetings a year, including an annual meeting on economic and social matters in the Spring, giving it a fixed venue consolidates the European Council's position as the body driving the Union's political agenda. Others, however, have regretted the fact that basing the European Council in Brussels might render the Union even remoter from citizens by removing a regular opportunity to bring 'the Union' to the 'member states' in a very visible way. It should be noted, however, that the declaration only refers to official meetings of the European Council, and does not apply to informal meetings which have been taking place with increasing frequency in recent years.

Role of the European Judicial Cooperation Unit (Eurojust)

Eurojust is a unit composed of national prosecutors and magistrates (or police officers of equivalent competence) detached from each member state which the Tampere European Council decided to set up in October 1999. At present the interim unit is based in the Council Secretariat. At French instigation (IGC 2000i), the treaty has included an express reference to Eurojust in Article 30 TEU along with a new paragraph 2 in Article 31 TEU. This will enable the Council to promote cooperation through Eurojust in facilitating proper coordination between member states' national prosecuting authorities and to promote support by Eurojust for criminal investigations in cases of serious cross-border crime. It will also foster cooperation between Eurojust and the European Judicial Network in order to facilitate the execution of letters rogatory and extradition requests.

Status of Interinstitutional Agreements

Interinstitutional Agreements (IIAs) are a form of 'soft law' which are political declarations subscribed to by the three main policy-making institutions. At the Commission's instigation, a declaration on IIAs was agreed explicitly, recalling that the duty of cooperation laid down in Article 10 TEC also governs relations between the Community institutions, and that IIAs are concluded in the context of that duty of cooperation to facilitate the application of the provisions of the TEC. The declaration recalls the fact that such agreements may not amend or supplement the provisions of the Treaties and stipulates that they may only be concluded with the agreement of these three institutions. Although this declaration does not enshrine IIAs as an instrument in the treaty, this can be seen as an institutional 'rebalancing' measure designed to clarify their status and give a clear political signal that all three of the institutions mentioned must be parties to them. In other words, IIAs cannot be concluded between the Commission and the Parliament alone without the Council as a party.

Legal Basis for the Social Protection Committee

Following a proposal by Ireland (IGC 2000f), a new Article 144 provides a treaty basis for establishing a Social Protection Committee, which is modelled on the Employment Committee foreseen in Article 130. This proposal was not controversial in its content since it secured a treaty basis for the Committee which already exists, thereby placing it on a firmer footing. However, explicitly mentioning it in the treaty reflects a worrying trend towards increasing compartmentalization of work within the Council, in particular through the proliferation of treaty-based Committees, which runs counter to the desire to enhance the overall coherence of work in the Council by limiting the number of Council formations and strengthening the role of COREPER in the Council's preparatory work as part of the process of equipping the Council for enlargement.

Position of the Community in Bodies Set Up by an Agreement with Third Countries

In order to lay down a coherent procedure for establishing the Community position each time decisions having legal effect have to be adopted by bodies set up under international agreements with third states by the Union, the Conference agreed to amend Article 300(2) in order to align the procedure with that currently used for association agreements.

Title of the *Official Journal*

Given that the *Official Journal*, in which all EU legislation and decisions are publicized before entering into force, publishes acts relating to all three pillars of the Union's activities, it appeared anomalous to still refer to it as the *Official Journal of the European Communities*. The four references to the *Official Journal* in the treaty (in Articles 248(1) and (4) and 254(1) and (2)) therefore had to be amended to rename it the *Official Journal of the European Union*.

Responses to Written Requests to EU Institutions and Bodies

Article 21 TEC establishes a right for every citizen of the Union to write to any of the Union's institutions or bodies in one of the official languages and to have an answer in the same language. Belgium suggested amending this article to ensure that an answer to any written request would be given within a reasonable period, mainly for internal domestic reasons presumably because of the fact that replies in Dutch (which would in many cases need to be translated) tended to be less rapidly forthcoming than replies in French. Since the institutions considered it self-evident that they would always endeavour to reply to requests in a reasonable period, a declaration (rather than a treaty amendment) was agreed to this effect.

Protocol on the Financial Consequences of the ECSC Treaty

In anticipation of the expiry of the European Coal and Steel Community on 23 July 2002, legal clarification was required in the treaty of the status of ECSC funds. A protocol has accordingly been annexed to the treaty to transfer all assets and liabilities to the European Community on 24 July 2002, to establish the use to which the assets will be put (research in sectors related to the coal and steel industry) and to provide a legal basis for the Council to adopt the essential principles and decision-making procedures for adopting multiannual financial guidelines for managing these assets under the relevant research programme.

9 |

Charting the Union's Future

The Treaty of Nice marks the completion of the structural renovations deemed necessary by the Union to allow more residents to be accommodated. All that remains is some internal refurbishment in advance of enlargement (see below). No government harboured more ambitious expectations for the treaty, although certain sections of the media appeared to consider that the treaty should have at least begun to address some of the bigger questions about the purpose and end-goal of the Union. The reason was that away from the IGC negotiating rooms, nearly every European leader was expounding their thoughts on and vision for the future development of the Union. This debate was ignited by the speech delivered by the German Foreign Minister, Joschka Fischer, at the Humboldt University in Berlin on 12 May 2000 in which he set out his views on the aim of European integration. While it was never the intention for the Nice IGC to address these questions, it was clear that for some governments a successful outcome at Nice was contingent on a commitment to carry this debate forward into a more wide-ranging treaty reform exercise.

There were probably two key concerns behind the push for a new IGC in 2004. This first was the fact that in the face of large-scale expansion of the Union, some governments, including those advocating a more ambitious agenda at the outset (see Chapter 2) considered more was needed in order to secure further deepening of the integration process. The second was a concern about a lack of legal certainty and democratic legitimacy afforded by the Union's constitutional and institutional setup, reflected in the German call for a 'catalogue of competences' to better define the responsibilities of the different layers of government in the Union. This debate found tangible expression in the declaration on the future of the Union included in the Conference's final act (see Box 9.1). The declaration calls for further architectural adjustments not in order to deal with enlargement, but to improve and to monitor the democratic legitimacy and transparency of the Union and its institutions. Underlying this objective are concerns about the ability to sustain public support for the Union in general, and enlargement in particular. Opinion polls which show that less than three in ten Europeans believe welcoming new member states should be a priority for the Union are far from encouraging (Commission 2000c).

Two pitfalls need to be avoided in any debate on the future of the Union. First, the substance of the debate about the nature and organization of the Union needs to be separated from questions about the textual form, constitutional or otherwise, which might underpin it. Secondly, because many labels such as 'federalism' and 'constitution' have become highly emotive terms of political abuse, it is vital to deconstruct the often deliberately confusing rhetoric of the political debate and analyse what is actually being said. Clarity of concepts and objectives will be a *sine qua non* for successfully carrying forward the debate over the coming years. One thing at least is clear. As currently constituted, the EU does not possess the attributes of what is usually understood as a genuine federal state system, nor the potential to develop into such. The creation of a federal state structure, even if it were to remain a Union among distinct peoples and distinct political identities, would require unanimous agreement among all national governments and national parliaments, and probably electorates as well—an unlikely prospect. Even the most radical of the suggestions for reorganizing the basis of the Union take as a starting point the dual legitimacy underlying it: a Union of peoples (in the plural) and a Union of states. Jacques Delors and Joschka Fischer both speak in terms of 'a federation of nation States'. For Jacques Chirac, nations will remain the primary reference point for citizens. President Prodi also acknowledges this dual legitimacy based on the member states and the peoples of Europe. The idea of a European federal government for a 'super-state' subsuming the member states and merging their peoples into a single demos is therefore beyond reality.

This chapter considers four broad questions. First, it briefly recalls the need to pursue internal institutional reforms for enlargement as an important complement to the structural changes agreed in the Treaty of Nice. Second, it analyses the content of the Nice declaration on the future of the Union and outlines possible aspects of that debate. Third, it considers questions of procedure relating to the process launched at Nice. Finally, it looks at what the end product might be. This chapter will not analyse constitutional theory or the nature of the Union as a polity, on which a vast body of academic literature exists (see Weiler 1999, 2000; Burgess 2000), nor does it suggest a theoretical framework for a more precise division of powers between the various levels of government in the Union (see, for example, Pernice 2000). It more modestly outlines some of the parameters of the political debate and the problems of approaching and managing such a discussion in the Union in the years ahead. With such a potentially wide-ranging and complex agenda, it will be important to find common ground in understanding the different levels and layers of problems if meaningful political debate is to be conducted. Getting all participants in the debate to talk about the same thing at the same time will be a challenge in itself.

Internal Institutional Reforms

Essential as treaty reforms are for establishing the institutional ground-rules, it is equally imperative that day-to-day habits, customs and working methods in the Union's institutions are tailored to the operational requirements of a Union double its present size. All institutions are currently engaged in an internal reform process that will extend over the coming years. However, the Council will probably feel the impact of enlargement more keenly than the others. The European Parliament can deploy all the tools of a deliberative assembly which should enable it to adapt its working methods to cope with a modest increase in size, although growing to 732 members or more will make significant financial demands on its administrative budget. As far as the Commission is concerned, it has the certainty that its size is capped for the future. Full use will need to be made of the new provisions in the Treaty of Nice, particularly strengthened powers for the president. Furthermore, the Commission should benefit from improved internal organization following the substantial reform programme embarked on after the mass resignation of commissioners in 1999.

The Council, however, is most in need of overhaul. Its methods of work and negotiation are more akin to those of a diplomatic conference than a supranational legislative and executive body, and have changed relatively little since the Union's inception. Enlargement will force a radical change in working methods. This process has already started in 1999 with a report produced by the Council's secretary-general (the Trumpf-Piris report) (Council 1999a) which prompted some modest operational improvements agreed at the Helsinki European Council in December 1999 (Council 1999e). The structure, organization and methods of work of the Council's preparatory bodies, with new military and civilian crisis management structures adding a further layer of potential complexity, will need further revamping to ensure better coherence. Moreover, a number of intractable logistical problems will now have to be seriously addressed. Further work will continue throughout 2001 aimed at enhancing the continuity of Council presidencies, at distinguishing more clearly between its government/ executive and legislative functions, and at looking again at the way in which the Council handles and coordinates horizontal internal issues— a role for which the General Affairs Council at present appears ill-suited. Whatever is decided in this regard will probably have an impact on the conduct of the IGC foreseen for 2004.

The Declaration on the Future of the Union

The declaration on the future of the Union adopted in Nice (see Box 9.1) contains points relating to the substance and the procedure of the process which will ultimately lead to a further IGC in 2004. A 'deeper and wider debate about the future development of the European Union' has been launched. The stated purpose of this debate is to 'improve and to monitor the democratic legitimacy and transparency of the Union and its institutions to bring them closer to the citizens of the Member states'. In considering these, questions about the Union's very purpose are likely to be raised.

   The question of the Union's ultimate political goal and constitutional settlement has given rise to an intractable debate pitting federalists against intergovernmentalists since the 1950s. Federalists typically see this process ultimately culminating in some sort of central government and legislature. The trouble with the word 'federalism', as Finnish Prime Minister Paavo Lipponen put it in his Bruges speech on 10 November 2000, is that 'it means different things to different people. For some it means centralisation of powers, for others it is about decentralisation based on the principle of subsidiarity and a clear separation of powers. Both are right'. Many Eurosceptics, on the other hand, would like to backtrack and confine the Union to an intergovernmentally organized free trade area along the model of NAFTA, fostering competition in a single market, while forgetting that the Union is

Box 9.1: Declaration on the future of the Union

1. Important reforms have been decided in Nice. The Conference welcomes the successful conclusion of the Conference of Representatives of the Governments of the Member States and commits the Member States to pursue the early ratification of the Treaty of Nice.
2. It agrees that the conclusion of the Conference of Representatives of the Governments of the Member States opens the way for enlargement of the European Union and underlines that, with ratification of the Treaty of Nice, the European Union will have completed the institutional changes necessary for the accession of new Member States.
3. Having thus opened the way to enlargement, the Conference calls for a deeper and wider debate about the future of the European Union. In 2001, the Swedish and Belgian Presidencies, in cooperation with the Commission and involving the European Parliament, will encourage wide-ranging discussions with all interested parties: representatives of national parliaments and all those reflecting public opinion, namely political, economic and university circles, representatives of civil society, etc. The candidate States will be associated with this process in ways to be defined.
4. Following a report to be drawn up for the European Council in Göteborg in June 2001, the European Council, at its meeting in Laeken/Brussels in December 2001, will agree on a declaration containing appropriate initiatives for the continuation of this process.
5. The process should address, inter alia, the following questions:
   - how to establish and monitor a more precise delimitation of powers between the European Union and the Member States, reflecting the principle of subsidiarity;
   - the status of the Charter of Fundamental Rights of the European Union, proclaimed in Nice, in accordance with the conclusions of the European Council in Cologne;
   - a simplification of the Treaties with a view to making them clearer and better understood without changing their meaning;
   - the role of national parliaments in the European architecture.
6. Addressing the abovementioned issues, the Conference recognises the need to improve and to monitor the democratic legitimacy and transparency of the Union and its institutions, in order to bring them closer to the citizens of the Member States.
7. After these preparatory steps, the Conference agrees that a new Conference of the Representatives of the Governments of the Member States will be convened in 2004, to address the abovementioned items with a view to making corresponding changes to the Treaties.
8. The Conference of Member States will not constitute any form of obstacle or pre-condition to the enlargement process. Moreover, those candidate States which have concluded accession negotiations with the Union will be invited to participate in the Conference. Those candidate States which have not concluded their accession negotiations shall be invited as observers.

as much a political as an economic project. This 'thus-far-and-no-further' view also conveniently overlooks the fact that even standstill in a functioning single market requires a process of continual regulation as technology advances and standards of health and safety evolve over time. While the lack of a clearly defined political finishing line has not impeded the Union's development over the past 50 years, the question is whether defining such a goal is a necessary condition for sustaining support for the Union in future.

The onward march towards 'ever closer Union' can be viewed in two diametrically opposing ways. It can be considered an essential factor providing the dynamic for the European Union and ensuring momentum towards deeper integration, both by encouraging the Union to use its existing powers to the full, and legitimizing the extension of the limits of these powers in successive IGCs. Alternatively, it is seen as an invitation for constant constitutional change as part of an inexorable and unstoppable process. Establishing definitively and unequivocally the Union's powers and responsibilities is accordingly viewed either as another decisive leap in the direction of closer integration, or as a means of setting clear limits to the process. Advocates can be found in both schools arguing that the Union's legitimacy depends on placing it on a stronger 'constitutional' foundation than at present, particularly if public support for both continued integration and enlargement is to be sustained. This throws up some rather fundamental political questions for the Union. First, is the successful development of the Union now predicated upon a clearer definition of the powers which it should exercise? If so, at how ambitious or modest a level should the limits of Union action be set in establishing a shareout of powers?

There are two reasons that might explain why the constitutional debate has gained momentum in parallel with the IGC. First, the fact that the Union in the not-too-distant future will have reached a size close to its geographical limits makes it all the more relevant to pose questions about its nature and purpose. Second, many feel that the Union has already advanced so far down the road of integration that the time has come for a qualitative change in its structures and methods both to improve democratic legitimacy and render it a viable and sustainable entity. This involves not only considering the scope and limits of the Union's powers (see below), but also the operating mode to be used in exercising them. In the present treaties, several different methods of operation exist side by side. Some view recourse to the so-called 'Community method' as the ideal to be extended to all areas of Union activity. Increasingly, the Union is resorting to hybrid methods such as those used for CFSP and cooperation in police and criminal law matters, as well as the so-called 'open method of coordination', involving benchmarking and measuring best practice through commonly agreed indicators and scoreboards to generate peer pressure. The Community method has certainly proved its worth; it is arguably the only effective way to operate when handling legislative matters inside the Union. However, it probably cannot offer a universal panacea. In future, as has been done in the Maastricht treaty, different operating modes for the Union need be considered on the basis of functional needs depending on the Union's objectives, areas and scope of action, rather than seen as an ideological shibboleth. Change in the way a particular method is used, however, can never be neutral, and necessarily has a knock-on effect on institutional relationships within the Union.

The declaration expressly mentions four subjects to be taken up in the debate: how to establish and monitor a more precise delimitation of powers between the European Union and the member states; the status of the Charter of Fundamental Rights; simplification of the treaties with a view to making them clearer and better understood without changing their meaning; and the role of national parliaments in the European architecture. Two general points are worth noting.

First, the exercise will not solely be limited to these four items, which are in any case cited as a non-exhaustive list. Given that the process will begin with wide-ranging discussions with all interested parties, including representatives of national parliaments, public opinion, political, economic and university circles and representatives of civil society, the debate is inevitably bound to range more widely. After launching such a broad-based debate, it would not make political sense to then seek to rein in the scope of work too far without having taken due account of the range of issues raised in the public debate. This means that everything is *potentially* negotiable in the process leading up to and during the 2004 IGC.

Second, while consideration could be given to each of the four items listed without altering substantially the *status quo* in terms of the share-out of powers between the Union and the member states or the present institutional balance, the declaration recognizes the need to 'improve and monitor the democratic legitimacy and transparency of the Union and its institutions to bring them closer to the citizens of the Member states'. This suggests that something needs to change, without determining the particular direction in which the Union should move. What this means in concrete terms will be determined during the process.

Establishing the basic framework for understanding the issues in conducting an organized political debate on such a diverse range of politically divisive and legally complex subjects is the main problem.

More Precise Delimitation of Powers
There are three reasons why this question has been posed with seemingly greater urgency as a backdrop to the IGC. First is the perception which has been growing over a number of years that a lack of legal certainty exists regarding the extent of the Union's powers. At the outset of the Community, a general tendency existed for the Union continually to seek to use treaty provisions as extensively as possible in activating its potential powers conferred by the treaties. This was considered legitimate use of the treaties (and still is by some, even if this practice is no longer current) given the injunction to 'continue the process of creating an ever closer Union'. Nevertheless, as long as any member state could veto action by the Community in important areas of policy, acting in this way appeared acceptable. However, with widespread recourse to QMV, individual governments no longer retain a final say over the extent to which the Union might exercise its potential powers. The feeling is growing in certain quarters that even if the Union has no ambition to evolve into a fully-fledged federation, it should *at the very least* offer its constituent parts (i.e. member states) similar levels of guarantee as offered by federal states to their constituent parts (Quermonne 1999). Second is ever-increasing pressure from sub-regional entities in member states (particularly in Germany) to recover some powers currently enshrined in the treaties which they regard as inappropriate for the Union to be exercising. This most frequently cited example is culture, which in many states is a responsibility fully devolved to sub-national entities. Although the Union's powers in this area are marginal, it has always been one area which has stubbornly resisted any move to QMV in successive IGCs for this very reason. The third and most fundamental reason is the desire by some to arrive at a final point of equilibrium between the powers of the Union and those of the member states, without the presumption that progress must always be made towards 'ever closer Union' (Patten 2000).

Delimiting powers between the Union and the member states is not just a simple matter of deciding which does what and drawing up a list of policy areas to be dealt with by the Union, with the remainder a matter for member states. Box 9.2 outlines possible angles for approaching the problem on the basis of the Union's existing powers by situating the various levels at which the debate will need to be conducted if it is to be undertaken seriously. If nothing else, it illustrates that the problem is complex and multi-layered.

First, there is the question of defining the *extent* of the Union's powers. The terms of this debate are slightly different depending on whether the matter debated falls within the EC or the EU Treaty. The EC Treaty is based on the principle of conferred powers with an established legal order for enforcing decisions. Under the EU Treaty, powers are conferred on the Union, although modes of decision-making and judicial coverage are very different. Leaving that difficulty aside, however, the extent of the Union's conferred powers can be determined in terms of policy areas (broadly or narrowly defined), in terms of general or specific objectives within any given policy area and by the degree to which the Union is empowered to intervene. The treaty defines Union powers in each of these three ways. At present the Union also foresees a variety of levels of intervention ranging from outright harmonization to cooperation. Clarifying the extent of the Union's competence will involve addressing all of these layers.

Second, there is the definition of the *nature* of the Union's powers. A basic distinction can be drawn between powers which are expressly conferred 'exclusively' to the Community under the treaty, that is, which rule out any possibility of intervention by member states unless expressly authorized by the Community, and powers which can be exercised by both the Community and the member states. The main area of exclusive powers 'reserved' to the Community in this way is the Common Commercial Policy under Article 133. In most other areas of policy, powers are said to be 'competing', that is, member states may act only to the extent to which the Union has not acted in the particular area in question. In some areas of course, the Union has acted to such an extent that member states' room for manoeuvre is practically non-existent. In such areas, the Community is also said to have exclusive competence (e.g. common market organizations under the CAP and the common fisheries policy). In areas where powers are competing, the Union cannot from day one exercise in full all the powers conferred on

Box 9.2: Approaching the problem of defining, exercising and monitoring the Union's powers

Possible angles for approaching the problem

Defining the extent of the Union's conferred powers *(Norms in the treaties—principle of conferral)*		
• **By area** Specific matter *or* entire sector • **By objective** Specific *or* general (i.e. Article 308) • **Degree of intervention** Harmonization/minimum rules/mutual recognition/coordination/incentive measures/cooperation, etc.		

Defining the nature of the Union's powers *(Definition in the treaties)*		
Express exclusive powers	**Competing powers** Actually 'activated'	**Competing powers** Potential

Exercising the Union's powers *(Principles/rules in the Treaties governing adoption of secondary legislation)*
• **Principle of subsidiarity** • **Principle of proportionality** • **Voting rules**: unanimity *or* QMV

Monitoring the Union's powers *(Procedures established in the Treaties)*
• **Political control *ex ante*** EU Institutions Ad hoc procedure/body involving national Parliaments? • **Judicial review *ex post*** ECJ National courts

Implementing Union action *(Responsibility established in the Treaties)*	
Responsibility of member states (general rule)	**Responsibility of the Union (exception)**

it; hence the distinction between powers which are 'actually activated' and 'potential' powers. Activation occurs once the Union adopts secondary legislation. For example, under the TEU, the Union's competence to act in foreign policy is virtually boundless. This is necessary given the nature of foreign policy. Article 11 TEU states that 'The Union shall define and implement a common foreign and security policy covering *all* areas of common and security policy' (emphasis added). In other words it has broad 'potential' powers but has only 'activated' them to a very limited extent as and when needs have arisen justifying action by the Union.

Third, there are the arrangements laid down in the treaties for *exercising* the powers conferred on the Union. It is at this level that the battleground in recent IGCs has been located. In exercising its powers, the Union can only act where powers have been explicitly conferred under the treaties and to the extent provided by the treaties (by objective or by area) under the principle of conferral. Article 308 TEC also allows action by the Community to attain an objective of the Community where no specific legal basis covering a specific area has been included in the treaty. For areas where powers are 'competing', the principles of subsidiarity and proportionality defined in Article 5 TEC and fleshed out in a treaty protocol must be respected. These principles mean that 'the Community shall take action only if and insofar as the objectives of the proposed action cannot be sufficiently achieved by the Member States and can therefore by reason of the scale of effects of the proposed action, be better achieved by the Community'. The principle of subsidiarity was introduced into the Treaty of Maastricht, and supplemented by the Protocol included in the Treaty of Amsterdam. It was not aimed at limiting the scope of the Union's powers, but to assist in determining where to place the dividing line between 'activated' and 'potential' powers in any particular policy area involving competing member state/Union powers. Proportionality determines the scale of action by the Union to ensure that sledgehammers are not used to crack nuts. It can also be used to determine the instrument the EU should deploy in order to achieve a particular objective in any given circumstances: some areas require hard law; in others 'soft' measures are sufficient. Both principles must necessarily be respected in any action undertaken by the Union. Finally, the voting rules laid down in the treaty governing the adoption of secondary legislation are also an important factor in determining the extent to which potential powers are exercised. The voting rules cannot themselves alter the nature of the powers, but have a significant bearing on the content of measures adopted by the Union (see Chapter 5). Attempts in future to provide a clearer definition of the scope of potential competence set out above would probably facilitate the transition to qualified majority voting.

Fourth, the treaties determine the ways in which the Union's powers, and hence the application of the various principles outlined above, are *monitored*. This occurs in two layers. First as an integral part of the policy-making process before decisions are taken. At present verification in respect of the principles of subsidiarity and proportionality is carried out by the Union's policy-making institutions in the course of discussion of legislative proposals, since the Protocol lays down obligations incumbent on the Commission, the Council and the European Parliament. Suggestions have been made to create *ad hoc* procedures for verifying compliance or to confer the task to a specific *ad hoc* body. After acts have been adopted, monitoring whether the Union has acted in accordance with the treaties becomes a matter for judicial review.

Fifth, *implementation* of policies decided by the Union is carried out for the most part by member states, and only to a marginal extent by the administrative authorities of the Union itself. One of the features of the Union has been the relatively small size of its central bureaucracy which is smaller than that needed to run a medium-sized city. This is because member states have assumed the bulk of responsibility for implementation of Union's policies, with the Commission, as guardian of the treaties, ensuring that they fulfil the responsibilities and obligations conferred on them.

In previous IGCs, work focused mainly on the way in which the Union exercises and monitors its powers (points three and four above). In the past, member states have been reluctant to enter into an explicit discussion about delimiting the Union's powers more clearly. IGCs have typically either simply added new policy areas into the treaties, or limited the degree of intervention permissible for the Union—for example by explicitly ruling out harmonization on certain areas. Entering into a real debate on the first two of the points above inevitably raises the question of fixing a final end goal for the Union. The key question is whether fixing such a definitive point of equilibrium between the Union and the member states means abandoning the mantra of 'ever closer Union'. Removing this objective would depend on the nature and ambition of the settlement reached in the next IGC.

Choices exist regarding the purpose and level of ambition for a share-out of powers between the Union and the member states and the structure of the EU's institutions. It is readily acknowledged that many of society's intractable problems no longer respect borders and therefore cannot be adequately addressed by individual member states on their own. Creating a clean environment, combating international organized crime, stemming illegal migration flows and guaranteeing food safety can only be seriously addressed on a continent–wide or even broader basis. Mounting operations such as those in Kosovo can only be done successfully as part of a combined effort. Accepting this logically implies giving the Union real powers in such areas to the extent necessary for effective action. Already the treaties have given considerable powers to the Union in monetary policy and extensive potential competence in foreign policy and internal security. These powers have only been exercised to any significant extent in the monetary policy area, although an evolution has already begun in the other two areas. The counterpart to any such movement has to be strict application of the principles of subsidiarity and proportionality, with the Union refraining from regulating matters where little justification exists for it to do so, and which only serve to alienate businesses and citizens, and further weaken the case for common action when such action is needed. Entering into such a complex legal and political mine-field nevertheless involves the evident risk of member states seeking to claw back certain competences which they consider inappropriate for the Union to exercise for legal/constitutional reasons or to satisfy domestic presures or public opinion.

Status of the Charter of Fundamental Rights for the European Union
This Charter was solemnly proclaimed at Nice setting out in visible form the fundamental rights guaranteed by the Union. Many delegations were open to proclaiming the Charter in a legally binding form. Given reluctance on the part of a number of member states, in particular Denmark, the UK and Ireland, the Charter was not incorporated into the Treaty of Nice as a legally binding text, but proclaimed as a political statement. The question as to whether the Charter would be incorporated into any future treaty or not is left open as a point to be considered in 2004. Technically, this point does not pose any particular practical difficulties since the text of the Charter already exists—what is now done with it is largely a political question.

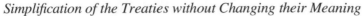

Simplification of the Treaties without Changing their Meaning

At face value, this involves a simple tidying-up exercise to reorder nearly 800 articles in the dozen or so existing basic treaties and acts in a more user-friendly, easily digestible and comprehensible form. The Amsterdam IGC removed many obsolete provisions, but reordering or merging the treaties was considered too ambitious, in particular because of potential political difficulties in re-ratifying the treaties in many member states. An unofficial consolidation was carried out following the Amsterdam IGC (Council 2000b), and suggestions have been made in 2000 by the European University Institute in Florence (EUI 2000; Commission 2000d). While simplification and reorganization of the treaties (including possibly merging the EC and EU Treaties) may be a laudable exercise in itself, it opens up the possibility of separating fundamental and constitutional provisions from those relating to policy detail. The debate on simplification will require clarification as to what precisely the scope or level of ambition of the exercise should be: simply to make the treaties easier to understand; to change their structure; or to enable the use of different procedures for amending different parts of the treaties —for example, a 'heavy' procedure for the fundamental provisions and some 'lighter' procedure for provisions on policies. Such an exercise is both technically complex and also has far-reaching political and psychological implications, depending on the ultimate status and denomination given to the document which results from the IGC in 2004.

Role of National Parliaments

The role of national parliaments in the European architecture has been a long-running debate since Maastricht and Amsterdam (which resulted in a treaty protocol on the subject) and has been revived in some of the statements made in parallel to the IGC calling for a second parliamentary chamber to be established composed of representatives of national parliaments. National parliaments are of course involved in the approval of primary legislation in the Union and play an important role regarding the choice of form and methods for transposing the results to be achieved by EC directives into national legislation. However, the role played by national parliaments in calling government ministers to account before decisions are taken in the Council varies considerably from one member state to another. In some states such as Denmark, government ministers operate on a tight rein from the Parliament. In others, parliamentary scrutiny is weak. At present the only role foreseen for national parliaments under the treaty are the arrangements which have been put in place under the Protocol on national parliaments, which has enhanced the advisory role of the Conference of European Affairs Committees of national parliaments and the European Parliament (COSAC), and fixes a minimum six-week delay between a Commission legislative proposal being tabled and adoption of the act or the common position by the Council.

There are probably limits to how one political system (the European Union) can be democratized through the institutions of another (the nation-state) (Lord 1998). The difficulty is how to resolve the problem of providing effective accountability where the task of government at the level of the Union is shared by member state governments and the Commission. Heads of government in the European Council and national government ministers in the Council are subject to political scrutiny on an individual basis, with widely varying degrees of effectiveness, by each national parliament. While a few might argue that some form of *collective* accountability of the Council to a representative assembly is desirable, this is a false problem. Collective accountability of the Council to any such body, or any other body for that matter, involving the possibility of national ministers being forced to resign, is entirely at odds with the notion of the Union as a 'Union of states' each with its own democratically elected and legitimate government. However, just because the Council cannot formally be made collectively accountable to a parliamentary chamber does not mean that it should not work subject to the approval of a parliament in adopting legislation. This already happens under the codecision procedure. That QMV in the Council for legislative matters has largely been coupled with codecision does not fully resolve the problem when the Council is acting outside the scope of codecision. If a second parliamentary chamber were to perform some legislative function, this would place a question mark over the Council's legislative role. If, on the other hand, such a second chamber were conceived as a body monitoring whether the Union's powers are being exercised in accordance with the principles laid down in the treaties, its role would be very different. Many proponents of a second EP chamber see it fulfilling this latter purpose. Whatever its function, any decision to set up of a second parliamentary chamber would represent a major shift in the roles of the Union's institutions with far-reaching implications for the European Parliament, the Council and the Commission.

Given the originality of the European Union as a polity, the task will be to find the most effective way in which control and accountability by both national parliaments and the European Parliament can complement one another. All too often, they are seen as competing rather than complementary. This is because behind many of the debates regarding the so-called democratic deficit levelled at the European institutions lies the classic debate between integration and intergovernmental cooperation that has marked each stage of the European enterprise. In other words, in this debate the issue is less about democracy than about the way the European Union is envisaged (de Schoutheete 2000).

Procedure for Carrying Forward the Process

In the light of the experience of negotiating the Treaty of Nice, a head of steam has built up in favour of broadening the process of negotiating the next treaty revision. In the process just launched, two things seem certain. First, there will be a wide-ranging debate with all interested parties in 2001 about the future development of the European Union launched by the Swedish and Belgian presidencies in cooperation with the Commission and involving the European Parliament. Second, in 2004 there will be an Intergovernmental Conference to examine amendments to the treaties. What happens in 2002 and 2003 still has to be defined. This is where possible innovative approaches could be tested for preparing the IGC. This will be clearer in the declaration containing appropriate initiatives for the continuation of the process to be agreed at the Laeken-Brussels European Council in December 2001.

Many heads of government have suggested, or not ruled out, the formula of the Convention used to negotiate the Charter of EU Fundamental Rights for all or part of this intermediate preparatory phase of work. The Convention was composed of representatives of all national parliaments, the European Parliament, national governments and the European Commission (see Appendix 4). However, the fact that the Convention was a successful formula for the Charter does not necessarily mean that it is the body best suited to carry out the Conference's preparatory work in exactly the same form. First, the subject matter handled by an IGC is quite different from that in a fundamental rights Charter. The latter was limited to a clearly definable agenda, with disputes being contained to the margins of the principles participants wished to put beyond politics by including them in the Charter.

Preparing the next IGC involves a much broader agenda dealing with a vast array of issues, many of which are at the heart of government in the Union. Second, given that representatives from candidate states' governments and national parliaments would be involved, the body would increase substantially in size. Although not a panacea for preparing negotiations on constitutional change in the Union, there is no reason why it would not be possible to tailor the Convention formula in any number of ways into an instrument which can effectively prepare an IGC. One potential advantage of such an approach is that it would probably ensure that the forthcoming IGC has available at the start of its work a complete series of texts and options, rather than having to draw them up itself from scratch in the course of proceedings. However, this alone would not be sufficient to guarantee an efficient IGC without a number of other measures (see Chapter 2).

The End Product

While some are keen to see the process culminate in a 'constitution', a semantic debate on the nature of the final document would be unproductive until the substance of the agenda has been clarified. The question of the form and denomination of the final document, while it might be an ancillary question in strictly legal terms, is one which has huge political and psychological implications, even if the reality matters more than the label. A healthy measure of caution needs to be exercised in using labels such as 'constitution' to describe the form to be given to any finished document (Piris 1999). The term unfortunately has 'superstate' connotations, particularly in the UK. British political philosophers, apart from distinguished exceptions such as William Penn and Jeremy Bentham, brought up in a system of government without a written constitutional document, have not generally wished to foist one on Britain or on the rest of Europe. As Tony Blair pointed out 'it is perhaps easier for the British than for others to recognise that a constitutional debate must not necessarily end with a single, legally binding document called a constitution' (Warsaw speech, October 2000). However, between the term 'treaty' (which is what in legal terms the outcome of the next IGC will be) and 'constitution', there is a range of possible denominations and titles which could be given to such a text. Changing the name of the final document would signal an end to the continual process of treaty revision in which negotiations on the next treaty are already programmed before the ink is even placed on the one which has just been negotiated. Finding a denomination other than 'treaty', which suggests a transient agreement, but avoiding the word 'constitution', would convey the idea that the construction is a durable one, but not one in which the member states are subordinated to or subsumed into the Union. If a functional approach is followed towards the whole question of defining the Union's powers and its modes of operation in different areas, the semantic problem should at least be placed in perspective.

Concluding Remarks

The process leading to 2004 does not constitute any form of obstacle or pre-condition to enlargement, and it is one in which candidate states will be closely involved. It is impossible to predict whether participants preparing and negotiating the next treaty revision in 2004 will succeed in the task which has been set at Nice, or even whether serious attempts will be made to grapple with the full implications of the points expressly mentioned in the Nice declaration. At least the conditions have been created for them to do so by defining the basic terms of reference in sufficiently broad terms for an ambitious exercise, by allowing sufficient time for proper debate and by calling for as broad a participation as possible in the process. The difficulty in any debate such as this, dealing with the balance between the member states and the Union, and between the institutions, is that it goes to the very heart of the purpose of and ambitions for the European Union. Viable blueprints cannot ignore the nature of the Union is an entirely novel kind of political association with its own constitutional system. Much will depend on the political context in which this debate is conducted. There has to be good reasons to tinker with the fundamental features of a mechanism which has already achieved much. Weiler, though not opposed to improving the treaties or the Union's institutional arrangements, urges caution. As he puts it: 'Europe has charted its own brand of constitutional federalism. It works. Why fix it?' (Weiler 2001).

10 |

Realities and Illusions in Perspective

Heads of state and government were faced with an unenviable task in Nice. Issues involving the carve-up of power or financial resources inside the Union inevitably result in divisive wrangling, particularly when the negotiating base is as narrowly defined and room for trade-offs as limited as they were in Nice. The last time heads of government found themselves negotiating through the night was in agreeing Agenda 2000 at the Berlin European Council in March 1999 (Galloway 1999). The Nice IGC negotiations resembled those on Agenda 2000 in three respects. First, the issues were complex and they mattered; this partly explains why the final political deal brokering took so long. Second, issues of public presentation were an important factor in determining the final outcome; this explains the need for presentational artifices and confirms that negotiations in the EU cannot be understood in isolation from the domestic political context in member states. Third, as is always the case, the presidency had to pay a price in giving ground on strong national positions in order to secure agreement. This is a positive factor for the Union, since it is practically impossible for presidencies to foist their own outcome onto unwilling heads of government.

Overall Assessment of the Treaty of Nice

The Treaty of Nice had a difficult birth. Announced in the press as the ailing child of quarrelsome parents, the omens did not bode well. However, the progeny seems to be improving with age. It is always difficult to arrive at a balanced assessment of any treaty in the immediate aftermath of its negotiation. Assessments in the emotion of the moment often fail to grasp the full significance of what has been agreed. The following quotation sums up much of the press reporting on the Treaty of Nice, as a treaty 'clearly the result of a confrontational negotiation in which the participants sought diametrically opposing objectives, the outcome of which was cobbled together any old how so as not to give the impression of failure'. Only this quotation referred not to the Treaty of Nice but to the Single Act in 1986 and was made by the distinguished former ECJ judge and diplomat Pierre Pescatore (Pescatore 1986). A balanced appraisal of the Treaty of Nice was made more difficult because of the searing indictment by the press of the presidency's handling of the Conference which was transposed to the content of the Treaty itself. This overshadowed the achievement of striking the final deal. Many of the realities had to be discerned by peeling away illusions, both positive in that they facilitated agreement (in the case of Commission size), and negative in that they lacked transparency without necessarily facilitating agreement (in the case of vote weighting). Understanding the Treaty of Nice thus requires the ability to distinguish between reality and illusion. The inability to do so in the immediate aftermath of Nice explains why many found it so difficult to get a clear picture of what had been agreed.

The preceding chapters have highlighted in each case the plusses and minuses contained in the treaty. Once they are added up, the overall balance sheet is a positive one, with which most candidate states appear to be satisfied.

First of all, the very existence of an agreement will, once it has been ratified, have removed the last remaining internal barrier on the Union's side for enlargement to proceed. Failure to agree would have been disastrous, not only in terms of the timetable for enlargement but in terms of the impact inside the Union, both on the euro and on the mood among heads of government who would not have relished the prospect of another round on these divisive issues at some later date. Once the negotiation went into Sunday, heads of state and government were virtually condemned to succeed. The consequences of failure would have been far more politically damaging.

Second, the criticism levelled at the treaty in certain quarters 'for failing to address some of the fundamental questions about the Union's end goal raised by heads of government during the year was unwarranted. There was never any question during the Conference of the Treaty of Nice tackling these broader issues. It would certainly have been remarkable had the Treaty come up with answers to questions which were not even on the table! These questions have now been posed in the declaration on the future of the Union to be examined up to and during the next IGC which will take place in 2004.

Third, the Treaty contains a number of improvements. On the size and composition of the Commission, the outcome was better than most had anticipated. Capping the future size of the Commission represents a significant step forward in ensuring its strength and independence for the future. The future appointment of the president of the Commission by QMV was undoubtedly one of the positive surprises from Nice. The fact that around 40 provisions will shift to QMV is a politically credible outcome, albeit tempered by lack of progress on social security coordination and taxation due to objections by a small number of delegations. That recourse has been made to transitional periods in a limited number of cases does not invalidate this conclusion. The key point is that, in most cases, the passage to QMV will occur automatically without necessitating further decisions. Skilful negotiation ensured that the treaty provisions transforming enhanced cooperation into a potentially usable instrument and altering the Union's judicial architecture were largely completed before Nice. Other important results include the introduction of an early warning procedure in Article 7 TEU where a clear risk exists of a breach of fundamental rights; and the changes allowing the Council to devolve operational political control and strategic guidance of crisis management operations to the Political and Security Committee.

For the European Parliament, the outcome, though not spectacular, consolidates its position as co-legislator. The European Parliament could not realistically expect to make comparable gains to those achieved at Maastricht and Amsterdam given that the Conference deliberately refrained from discussing any substantial alteration to the current institutional balance. Codecision has been extended to a number of new policy areas, and the Parliament has gained in terms of its legal standing before the Court as well as being given a right of initiation under Article 7 TEU in the event of the risk of a clear breach of fundamental rights by a member state. For the reasons explained in Chapter 6, the outcome on seat allocation could only be achieved by breaching the 700 member ceiling fixed at Amsterdam. The Parliament has been critical of being used as the 'loose change' for reaching overall agreement.

It is unavoidable in any discussion of power distribution among member states in the Union that attempts are made to identify 'winners' and 'losers'. Every head of government left Nice with a presentable outcome. The presidency did the deal, but paid a price in terms of giving ground on national positions (a fate which befalls most presidencies with something at stake in major negotiations). Its reputation was dented as a result of the public criticism of its handling of proceedings in Nice. Undoubtedly the Union has also paid a price, particularly on Council vote weighting, where the number of political constraints involved in the final equation ostensibly appeared to make decision-making more difficult with three necessary conditions for qualified majority decisions in the Council (majority of votes, majority of members and 62% of the population). The issue inevitably became the focus of media attention as a yardstick for assessing winners and losers in the Conference. Yet, as Chapter 4 explained, the issues were complex, and complicated further by the politics of political presentation. Managing the negotiation on vote weighting was inevitably going to be difficult, rendered more so by the need to balance the various political constraints bearing down on the negotiation. This contrasts sharply with the outcome achieved on the Commission because the presidency devised and executed an effective strategy. Although the voting system is undeniably more complicated, the actual extent to which decision-making may have been rendered more difficult is probably only marginal given that a large *versus* small split never occurs in reality and that most qualified majorities represent more than 62% of the Union population. The fact that so much of the negotiation on this issue involved working with extreme configurations of member states goes a considerable way to explaining this outcome. The most worrying aspect is the projected rise in the QMV threshold. The one redeeming feature is that this will remain negotiable in each treaty of accession.

Looking to the Future

EU treaties are neither intrinsically 'good' nor 'bad'. They constitute the response to the political questions being asked of them at any given point in time. Each new treaty represents a further step forward in shaping the Union into its own constitutional mould. The results at Nice were probably the best that could have been expected in the present political environment. It is likely that under the presidency of another state, even one dedicated to the European cause in the most altruistic way and freed of all domestic political distractions, the results would have been much the same (Moïsi 2001). Given the uncertainties of operating in a Union of 27 or more member states, governments clearly preferred in many cases the most conservative approach available. While it is impossible to speculate on how specific negotiating outcomes might otherwise have turned out, experience has shown that most participants closely involved in EU negotiations usually develop a feel for predicting the zone of final equilibrium, barring the odd unpleasant, as well as pleasant, surprise. The Treaty of Nice contains both; in that respect it is no different from any other EU treaty.

The next treaty negotiations in 2004 will be the culmination of a lengthy preparatory process involving a broader agenda and probably more negotiating participants. The Union will be facing a changed political reality. The distribution issues involved in delimiting the powers between the Union and the member states and the balance of influence between the different EU institutions will be very different from those considered during the Nice IGC, but probably equally divisive. The exercise on which the Union is embarking will lead to a substantial reworking of the treaty in form, if not in substance. There is a risk in embarking on a debate involving terms such as 'constitution' and 'federalism' that discussion might get bogged down in issues of presentation. However, there are signs that the debate is moving from semantics to substance. Even those advocating an ambitious agenda, such as Fischer, Delors and Prodi, no longer speak in terms of a 'European federation', but in terms of a 'federation of nation states'. This shift *is* significant. The key to success, as outlined in Chapter 9, will be the ability to set aside empty semantic arguments and to take a functional approach to what the Union should be doing to confront the challenges facing all European states. For each task, consideration needs to be given to the most effective way, be it the Community method or other methods, for achieving common objectives in any given area.

The ultimate challenge for budding constitutional architects is to design structures which, while not creating a super-state Union, clearly emphasize the fact that the Union is an integral part of the public and political life of member states and their peoples in every region and municipality. Anchoring the Union in the member states can only reinforce the sense that the European Union is 'us' rather than some extraneous entity divorced from reality in Edinburgh, Tampere or Naples. This involves finding satisfactory answers to questions about democratic authorization, representation, accountability and identity in the European context (Lord 1998). The forthcoming wide-ranging debate will provide an opportunity to rise above an existential and meaningless 'yes' or 'no' to Europe and consider in clear and possibly definitive terms what kind of Europe people want and for what purpose.

Appendix 1

Texts Relating to Enlargement

1.1   Protocol on the Enlargement of the European Union

THE HIGH CONTRACTING PARTIES

HAVE AGREED UPON the following provisions, which shall be annexed to the Treaty on European Union and to the Treaties establishing the European Communities:

ARTICLE 1
Repeal of the Protocol on the institutions

The Protocol on the institutions with the prospect of enlargement of the European Union, annexed to the Treaty on European Union and to the Treaties establishing the European Communities, is hereby repealed.

ARTICLE 2
Provisions concerning the European Parliament

1.   On 1 January 2004 and with effect from the start of the 2004–2009 term, in Article 190(2) of the Treaty establishing the European Community and in Article 108(2) of the Treaty establishing the European Atomic Energy Community, the first subparagraph shall be replaced by the following:

'The number of representatives elected in each Member State shall be as follows:

Belgium	22
Denmark	13
Germany	99
Greece	22
Spain	50
France	72
Ireland	12
Italy	72
Luxembourg	6
Netherlands	25
Austria	17
Portugal	22
Finland	13
Sweden	18
United Kingdom	72'

2.   Subject to paragraph 3, the total number of representatives in the European Parliament for the 2004–2009 term shall be equal to the number of representatives specified in Article 190(2) of the Treaty establishing the European Community and

in Article 108(2) of the Treaty establishing the European Atomic Energy Community plus the number of representatives of the new Member States resulting from the accession treaties signed by 1 January 2004 at the latest.

3.   If the total number of members referred to in paragraph 2 is less than 732, a *pro rata* correction shall be applied to the number of representatives to be elected in each Member State, so that the total number is as close as possible to 732, without such a correction leading to the number of representatives to be elected in each Member State being higher than that provided for in Article 190(2) of the Treaty establishing the European Community and in Article 108(2) of the Treaty establishing the European Atomic Energy Community for the 1999-2004 term.

The Council shall adopt a decision to that effect.

4.   By way of derogation from the second paragraph of Article 189 of the Treaty establishing the European Community and from the second paragraph of Article 107 of the Treaty establishing the European Atomic Energy Community, in the event of the entry into force of accession treaties after the adoption of the Council decision provided for in the second subparagraph of paragraph 3 of this Article, the number of members of the European Parliament may temporarily exceed 732 for the period for which that decision applies. The same correction as that referred to in the first subparagraph of paragraph 3 of this Article shall be applied to the number of representatives to be elected in the Member States in question.

ARTICLE 3
Provisions concerning the weighting of votes in the Council

1.   On 1 January 2005:
  (a) in Article 205 of the Treaty establishing the European Community and in Article 118 of the Treaty establishing the European Atomic Energy Community:
  (i) paragraph 2 shall be replaced by the following:

'2.   Where the Council is required to act by a qualified majority, the votes of its members shall be weighted as follows:

Belgium	12
Denmark	7
Germany	29
Greece	12
Spain	27
France	29
Ireland	7
Italy	29
Luxembourg	4
Netherlands	13

Austria	10
Portugal	12
Finland	7
Sweden	10
United Kingdom	29

Acts of the Council shall require for their adoption at least 169 votes in favour cast by a majority of the members where this Treaty requires them to be adopted on a proposal from the Commission.

In other cases, for their adoption acts of the Council shall require at least 169 votes in favour, cast by at least two-thirds of the members.'

(ii) the following paragraph 4 shall be added:

'4. When a decision is to be adopted by the Council by a qualified majority, a member of the Council may request verification that the Member States constituting the qualified majority represent at least 62% of the total population of the Union. If that condition is shown not to have been met, the decision in question shall not be adopted.'

(b) In Article 23(2) of the Treaty on European Union, the third subparagraph shall be replaced by the following text:

'The votes of the members of the Council shall be weighted in accordance with Article 205(2) of the Treaty establishing the European Community. For their adoption, decisions shall require at least 169 votes in favour cast by at least two-thirds of the members. When a decision is to be adopted by the Council by a qualified majority, a member of the Council may request verification that the Member States constituting the qualified majority represent at least 62% of the total population of the Union. If that condition is shown not to have been met, the decision in question shall not be adopted.'

(c) In Article 34 of the Treaty on European Union, paragraph 3 shall be replaced by the following:

'3. Where the Council is required to act by a qualified majority, the votes of its members shall be weighted as laid down in Article 205(2) of the Treaty establishing the European Community, and for their adoption acts of the Council shall require at least 169 votes in favour, cast by at least two-thirds of the members. When a decision is to be adopted by the Council by a qualified majority, a member of the Council may request verification that the Member States constituting the qualified majority represent at least 62% of the total population of the Union. If that condition is shown not to have been met, the decision in question shall not be adopted.'

2. At the time of each accession, the threshold referred to in the second subparagraph of Article 205(2) of the Treaty establishing the European Community and in the second subparagraph of Article 118(2) of the Treaty establishing the European Atomic Energy Community shall be calculated in such a way that the qualified majority threshold expressed in votes does not exceed the threshold resulting from the table in the Declaration on the enlargement of the European Union, included in the Final Act of the Conference which adopted the Treaty of Nice.

ARTICLE 4
Provisions concerning the Commission

1. From 1 January 2005 and with effect from when the first Commission following that date takes up its duties, Article 213(1) of the Treaty establishing the European Community and Article 126(1) of the Treaty establishing the European Atomic Energy Community shall be replaced by the following:

'1. The Members of the Commission shall be chosen on the grounds of their general competence and their independence shall be beyond doubt.

The Commission shall include one national of each of the Member States.

The number of Members of the Commission may be altered by the Council, acting unanimously.'

2. When the Union consists of 27 Member States, Article 213(1) of the Treaty establishing the European Community and Article 126(1) of the Treaty establishing the European Atomic Energy Community shall be replaced by the following:

'1. The Members of the Commission shall be chosen on the grounds of their general competence and their independence shall be beyond doubt.

The number of Members of the Commission shall be less than the number of Member States. The Members of the Commission shall be chosen according to a rotation system based on the principle of equality, the implementing arrangements for which shall be adopted by the Council, acting unanimously.

The number of Members of the Commission shall be set by the Council, acting unanimously.'

This amendment shall apply as from the date on which the first Commission following the date of accession of the twenty-seventh Member State of the Union takes up its duties.

3. The Council, acting unanimously after signing the treaty of accession of the twenty- seventh Member State of the Union, shall adopt:

— the number of Members of the Commission;
— the implementing arrangements for a rotation system based on the principle of equality containing all the criteria and rules necessary for determining the

composition of successive colleges automatically on the basis of the following principles:

(a) Member States shall be treated on a strictly equal footing as regards determination of the sequence of, and the time spent by, their nationals as Members of the Commission; consequently, the difference between the total number of terms of office held by nationals of any given pair of Member States may never be more than one;

(b) subject to point (a), each successive college shall be so composed as to reflect satisfactorily the demographic and geographical range of all the Member States of the Union.

4.   Any State which accedes to the Union shall be entitled, at the time of its accession, to have one of its nationals as a Member of the Commission until paragraph 2 applies.

1.2   Declaration No. 20 on the Enlargement of the European Union[1]

The common position to be adopted by the Member States at the accession conferences, as regards the distribution of seats at the European Parliament, the weighting of votes in the Council, the composition of the Economic and Social Committee and the composition of the Committee of the Regions will correspond to the following tables for a Union of 27 Member States.

1. The European Parliament

Member states	EP seats
Germany	99
United Kingdom	72
France	72
Italy	72
Spain	50
Poland	50
Romania	33
Netherlands	25
Greece	22
Czech Republic	20
Belgium	22
Hungary	20
Portugal	22
Sweden	18
Bulgaria	17
Austria	17
Slovakia	13
Denmark	13
Finland	13
Ireland	12
Lithuania	12
Latvia	8
Slovenia	7
Estonia	6
Cyprus	6
Luxembourg	6
Malta	5
Total	732

1.   The tables in this declaration take account only of those candidate countries with which accession negotiations have actually started.

2. The Weighting of Votes in the Council

Members of the Council	Weighted votes
Germany	29
United Kingdom	29
France	29
Italy	29
Spain	27
Poland	27
Romania	14
Netherlands	13
Greece	12
Czech Republic	12
Belgium	12
Hungary	12
Portugal	12
Sweden	10
Bulgaria	10
Austria	10
Slovakia	7
Denmark	7
Finland	7
Ireland	7
Lithuania	7
Latvia	4
Slovenia	4
Estonia	4
Cyprus	4
Luxembourg	4
Malta	3
Total	345

Acts of the Council shall require for their adoption at least 258 votes in favour, cast by a majority of members, where this Treaty requires them to be adopted on a proposal from the Commission.

In other cases, for their adoption acts of the Council shall require at least 258 votes in favour cast by at least two-thirds of the members.

When a decision is to be adopted by the Council by a qualified majority, a member of the Council may request verification that the Member States constituting the qualified majority represent at least 62% of the total population of the Union. If that condition is shown not to have been met, the decision in question shall not be adopted.

3. The Economic and Social Committee

Member States	Members
Germany	24
United Kingdom	24
France	24
Italy	24
Spain	21
Poland	21
Romania	15
Netherlands	12
Greece	12
Czech Republic	12
Belgium	12
Hungary	12
Portugal	12
Sweden	12
Bulgaria	12
Austria	12
Slovakia	9
Denmark	9
Finland	9
Ireland	9
Lithuania	9
Latvia	7
Slovenia	7
Estonia	7
Cyprus	6
Luxembourg	6
Malta	5
Total	344

4. The Committee of the Regions

Member States	Members
Germany	24
United Kingdom	24
France	24
Italy	24
Spain	21
Poland	21
Romania	15
Netherlands	12
Greece	12
Czech Republic	12
Belgium	12
Hungary	12
Portugal	12
Sweden	12
Bulgaria	12
Austria	12
Slovakia	9
Denmark	9
Finland	9
Ireland	9
Lithuania	9
Latvia	7
Slovenia	7
Estonia	7
Cyprus	6
Luxembourg	6
Malta	5
Total	344

1.3   Declaration No. 21 on the Qualified Majority Threshold and the Number of Votes for a Blocking Minority in the Context of Enlargement

Insofar as all the candidate countries listed in the Declaration on the enlargement of the European Union have not yet acceded to the Union when the new vote weightings take effect (1 January 2005), the threshold for a qualified majority will move, according to the pace of accessions, from a percentage below the current one to a maximum of 73,4%. When all the candidate countries mentioned above have acceded, the blocking minority, in a Union of 27, will be raised to 91 votes, and the qualified majority threshold resulting from the table given in the Declaration on enlargement of the European Union will be automatically adjusted accordingly.

Appendix 2

Extending Qualified Majority Voting[1]

2.1 Provisions for which Unanimity Will Be Abandoned on Entry into Force of the Treaty of Nice

2.2 Provisions to Move to Qualified Majority Voting at Various Dates Subsequent to the Entry into Force of the Treaty of Nice

2.3 Provisions Generally Acknowledged to Be Constitutional, Quasi-Constitutional or Organic because of the *Sui Generis* Nature of the Union

2.4 Other Treaty Provisions Requiring Unanimity in the Council or Common Accord of the Representatives of the Governments of the Member States

2.5 Article 133 TEC as Amended by the Treaty of Nice

1.   This appendix includes all treaty provisions which were *not* subject to QMV prior to the Treaty of Nice.

2.1 Provisions for which Unanimity Will Be Abandoned on Entry into Force of the Treaty of Nice[2]

A. EXTENSION OF QUALIFIED MAJORITY VOTING

1. Appointment of CFSP special representatives
   (Article 23(2) TEU)
2. Conclusion of international agreements on matters covered by Titles V and VI of the TEU for which a qualified majority is required for the adoption of internal decisions or measures
   (Article 24 TEU)
3. Procedure for establishing enhanced cooperation under Title VI of the TEU
   (Article 40a TEU)
4. Procedure for enhanced cooperation under the TEC
   (Article 11 TEC)
5. Incentive measures to combat discrimination
   (Article 13(2) TEC)*
6. Provisions facilitating the exercise of the right of citizens of the Union to move and reside within the territory of the Member States
   (Article 18 TEC)*
7. Criteria and mechanisms for determining the Member State responsible for considering asylum applications
   (Article 63(1)(a) TEC)[3]*
8. Minimum standards on reception of asylum seekers
   (Article 63(1)(b) TEC)[3]*
9. Minimum standards with respect to the qualification of third country nationals as refugees
   (Article 63(1)(c) TEC)[3]*
10. Minimum standards on procedures in Member States for granting or withdrawing refugee status
    (Article 63(1)(d) TEC)[3]*
11. Minimum standards for giving temporary protection to refugees
    (Article 63(2)(a) TEC)[3]
12. Measures improving and simplifying the system for cross-border service of judicial documents (except aspects relating to family law)
    (Article 65(a) TEC)*

2. Asterisks denote provisions for which the codecision procedure will apply.

3. Provided that the Council, acting unanimously in accordance with Article 67(1), has previously adopted Community legislation defining common rules and basic principles.

13. Measures promoting the compatibility of the rules applicable in the Member States concerning the conflict of laws and of jurisdiction (except aspects relating to family law)
    (Article 65(b) TEC)*
14. Measures eliminating obstacles to the good functioning of civil proceedings (except aspects relating to family law)
    (Article 65(c) TEC)*
15. Measures in the event of severe difficulties in the supply of certain products
    (Article 100(1) TEC)
16. Community financial assistance, under certain conditions, to a Member State which is in difficulties or is seriously threatened with severe difficulties caused by natural disasters or exceptional occurrences beyond its control
    (Article 100(2) TEC)
17. Decisions on the position of the Community at international level as regards issues of particular relevance to economic and monetary union and on its representation
    (Article 111(4) TEC)
18. Measures necessary for the rapid introduction of the single currency in Member States without a derogation
    (Article 123(4) TEC)
19. Negotiation and conclusion of international agreements on trade in services and trade-related aspects of intellectual property (subject to Article 133(6))
    (Article 133(5) TEC)
20. Measures to encourage cooperation between Member States, excluding any harmonization of the laws and regulations of the Member States, in the fields referred to in Article 137(1) except points (c), (d), (f) and (g).
    (Article 137(2) TEC, first indent)*
21. Measures supporting the action of Member States on industry matters
    (Article 157(3) TEC *
22. Specific actions for economic and social cohesion outside the structural funds
    (Article 159 TEC)*
23. Economic, financial and technical cooperation with third countries
    (new Article 181a TEC)
24. Approval of the Statute for Members of the European Parliament (except rules or conditions relating to the taxation of Members or former Members)
    (Article 190(5) TEC)
25. Laying down regulations governing political parties at European level
    (Article 191, second paragraph, TEC)*
26. Appointment of the Secretary-General and Deputy Secretary-General of the Council
    (Article 207(2) TEC)
27. Extension of the scope of Article 210 to cover the salaries, allowances and pensions of the Members and Registrar of the Court of First Instance
    (Article 210 TEC)

28. Nomination and appointment of the President of the Commission
    (Article 214 TEC)
29. Nomination and appointment of the members of the Commission
    (Article 214 TEC)
30. Filling a vacancy in the Commission caused by death or resignation
    (Article 215 TEC)
31. Approval of the Rules of Procedure of the Court of Justice
    (Article 223, sixth paragraph, TEC)
32. Approval of the Rules of Procedure of the Court of First Instance
    (Article 224, fifth paragraph, TEC)
33. Approval of the rules of procedure of judicial panels
    (Article 225, fifth paragraph)
34. Appointment of members of the Court of Auditors
    (Article 247(3) TEC)
35. Approval of the Rules of Procedure of the Court of Auditors
    (Article 248(4) TEC)
36. Appointment of members of the Economic and Social Committee
    (Article 259(1) TEC)
37. Appointment of members of the Committee of the Regions
    (Article 263 TEC)

B.   PROVISION SUBJECT TO A REINFORCED MAJORITY

38. Determination of a clear risk of a serious breach by a Member State of the
    principles mentioned in article 6(1) TEU
    (Article 7(1) TEU)

C.   PROVISIONS TO BE DELETED FOR WHICH UNANIMITY APPLIES

39. Decision to integrate the WEU into the European Union
    (Article 17(1), second subparagraph TEU)
40. Possibility of assigning to the Commission tasks in connection with the
    implementation of common measures, particularly as regards social security
    for migrant workers
    (old Article 144 TEC)

2.2 Provisions to Move to Qualified Majority Voting at Various Dates Subsequent to the Entry into Force of the Treaty of Nice[4]

41. Measures on the crossing of external borders establishing standards and procedures for carrying out checks on persons at such borders (as soon as agreement has been reached on the scope of the measures concerning the crossing by persons of the external borders of the Member States
(Article 62(2)(a))* [5]
42. Measures setting out the conditions under which nationals of third countries shall have the freedom to travel during a period of no more than three months
(Article 62(3) TEC)* [5]
43. Measures on illegal immigration and illegal residence
(Article 63(3)(b) TEC)* [5]
44. Measures to ensure cooperation between the relevant departments of the administrations of the Member States, and between those departments and the Commission, in the areas covered by Title IV
(Article 66 TEC)
45. Rules applicable to the structural funds
(Article 161, first subparagraph TEC)
46. Creation of a cohesion fund
(Article 161, second subparagraph, TEC)
47. Financial regulations
(Article 279(1)(a) TEC)
48. Rules concerning the responsibility of financial controllers, authorising officers and accounting officers and concerning appropriate arrangements for inspection
(Article 279(1)(b) TEC)

4.   Asterisks denote provisions for which the codecision procedure will apply.

5.   QMV for these provisions subject to a Council decision before 1 May 2004. For Article 62(2)(a), QMV and codecision is contingent on agreement on the scope of the measures concerning the crossing by persons of the external borders of the Member States of the European Union.

2.3   Provisions Generally Acknowledged to Be Constitutional, Quasi-Constitutional or Organic because of the *Sui Generis* Nature of the Union

A. PROVISIONS FOR WHICH THE TREATIES EXPRESSLY PROVIDE FOR THE ADOPTION OF A DECISION BY THE MEMBER STATES IN ACCORDANCE WITH THEIR RESPECTIVE CONSTITUTIONAL RULES

1. Common defence
    (Article 17(1), first subparagraph, TEU)
2. Establishment of Conventions under Title VI of the TEU
    (Article 34(2) TEU)
3. Communitarisation of areas covered by Title VI
    (Article 42 TEU)
4. Revision of the Treaties
    (Article 48 TEU)
5. Accession of a new Member State
    (Article 49 TEU)
6. Additional rights of citizenship
    (Article 22 TEC)
7. Uniform electoral procedure
    (Article 190(4) TEC)
8. Provisions to confer jurisdiction on the Court of Justice in disputes relating to the application of acts which create Community industrial property rights
    (Article 229a TEC)
9. Own resources
    (Article 269 TEC)

B. PROVISIONS WHICH, IN VIEW OF THE *SUI GENERIS* CHARACTER OF THE EUROPEAN UNION, MAY BE CONSIDERED QUASI-CONSTITUTIONAL

10. Replacement of the provisions of the Protocol on the excessive deficit procedure
    (Article 104(14) TEC)
11. Amendment of the Statute of the ESCB without a proposal from the ECB
    (Article 107(5) TEC)
12. Principles and rules for conferring implementing powers on the Commission
    (Article 202 TEC)
13. Decisions on the order of Council Presidencies
    (Article 203 TEC)

14. Alteration of the number of Members of the Commission
    (Article 213(1) TEC)
15. Increase in the number of Advocates-General
    (Articles 222 TEC)
16. Creation of judicial panels to hear at first instance certain classes of action
    (Article 225a TEC)
17. Statute of the Court of Justice
    (Article 245(2) TEC)
18. Commission's prerogatives: amendment of Commission proposal; second co-decision and cooperation readings after a negative opinion from the Commission
    (Article 250(1) TEC) (Article 251(3) TEC) (Article 252(e) TEC)
19. Rules governing languages of the institutions
    (Article 290 TEC)
20. Attaining an objective of the Community without provision of the necessary powers
    (Article 308 TEC)

C. PROVISIONS DEROGATING FROM NORMAL TREATY RULES

21. Not charging CFSP and JHA operational expenditure to the EC budget
    (Articles 28(3) and 41(3) TEU)
22. Measures constituting a step back as regards the liberalisation of the movement of capital to or from third countries
    (Article 57 TEC)
23. Measures constituting a step back as regards transport
    (Article 72 TEC)

D. PROVISIONS IN RESPECT OF WHICH THE RULE OF UNANIMITY ENSURES CONSISTENCY BETWEEN INTERNAL AND EXTERNAL DECISIONS

24. Conclusion of international agreements under Titles V and VI where unanimity is required for the adoption of internal decisions or measures
    (Article 24 TEU)
25. Conclusion of international agreements unanimously in areas in which unanimity is required for the adoption of internal rules
    (Articles 133(5) and 300(2) TEC)

2.4   Other Treaty Provisions Requiring Unanimity in the Council or Common Accord of the Representatives of the Governments of the Member States[6]

1. Serious breach by a Member State of the principles mentioned in Article 6(1)
    (Article 7(2) TEU)
2. CFSP decisions
    (Article 23(1) TEU)
3. Decisions on police and judicial cooperation
    (Article 34 TEU)
4. Action to combat discrimination
    (Article 13(1) TEC)
5. Detailed arrangements for exercising the right to vote and stand in EP and municipal elections
    (Article 19 TEC)
6. Measures in the field of social security
    (Article 42 TEC)*
7. Directives concerning the taking-up and pursuit of activities as self-employed persons
    (Article 47(2) TEC)*
8. Measures with a view to ensuring the absence of controls on persons when crossing internal borders
    (Article 61(2) TEC)[7]
9. Measures on refugees and displaced persons promoting a balance of effort between Member States
    (Article 63(2)(b) TEC)[7]
10. Measures on immigration policy
    (Article 63(3)(a) and (b) TEC)[7]
11. Measures defining the rights and conditions under which nationals of third countries who are legally resident in a Member State may reside in other Member States
    (Article 63(4) TEC)[7]
12. Measures in the field of judicial cooperation in civil matters with aspects relating to family law
    (Article 65 TEC)[7]

6.   It should be noted that a few of these provisions are outdated. Asterisks denote provisions for which the codecision procedure applies.

7.   At Nice, Heads of government included a declaration in the Final Act in which they agreed to make their best endeavours to move these areas, or parts of them, to QMV and codecision on 1 May 2004 or as soon as possible thereafter.

13. Decisions adapting the provisions concerning the powers of the Court of Justice in areas covered by Title IV of the TEC
    (Article 67(2), second indent)[7]

14. Application of provisions concerning the principles of the regulatory system for transport liable to have serious effects on the standard of living and employment
    (Article 71(2) TEC)

15. Compatibility of state aids derogating from Articles 87 or 89 with the common market
    (Article 88(2) TEC)

16. Harmonisation of legislation concerning turnover taxes, excise duties and other forms of indirect taxation
    (Article 93 TEC)

17. Directives for the approximation of laws, regulations or administrative provisions of the Member States as directly affect the establishment or the functioning of the common market
    (Article 94 TEC)

18. Conferring specific tasks on the ECB
    (Article 105(6) TEC)

19. Agreements and arrangements on an exchange rate system for the single currency
    (Article 111(1) TEC)

20. Appointment of members of the ECB
    (Article 112(2) TEC)

21. Appointment of the President of the EMI
    (Article 117(1) TEC)

22. Conferring upon the Emi other tasks for the preparation of the third stage of EMU
    (Article 117(7) TEC)

23. Rate at which the single currency will be substituted for the currency of a Member State (and other measures) abrogating a derogation
    (Article 123(5) TEC)

24. Conclusion of certain agreements relating to trade in services and trade-related aspects of intellectual property
    (Article 133(5) TEC)

25. Extension of the application of Article 133, paragraphs 1 to 4, to international agreements relating to intellectual property insofar as they are not covered by paragraph 5
    (Article 133(7) TEC)

26. Measures in areas of social policy listed in Article 137(1), points (c), (d), (f) and (g)
    (Article 137(2) TEC)

27. Decision to move to QMV and codecision in areas covered by Article 137(1)(d), (f) and (g)
    (Article 137(2) TEC)

28. Incentive measures, excluding any harmonisation of the laws and regulations of the Member States, in the cultural field
    (Article 151(5) TEC)*
29. Certain environmental provisions
    (Article 175(2) TEC)
30. Association agreements and economic, financial and technical agreements with candidate States
    (Article 181a(2) TEC)
31. Association of overseas countries and territories
    (Article 187 TEC)
32. Rules and conditions relating to the taxation of Members and former Members of the European Parliament
    (Article 190(5) TEC)
33. Decision not to fill a vacancy in the Commission
    (Article 215, second subparagraph)
34. Appointment of Judges and Advocates-General to the Court of Justice
    (Article 223 TEC)
35. Appointment of Judges of the Court of First Instance
    (Article 224 TEC)
36. Appointment of members of judicial panels
    (Article 225a TEC)
37. Decision to amend certain articles of the statute of the EIB
    (Article 266 TEC)
38. Determination of the methods and procedures whereby the budget revenue provided under own resources are made available to the Commission
    (Article 279(2) TEC)
39. Seat of the institutions
    (Article 289 TEC)
40. Modifications to the list of products covered by paragraph 1(b)
    (Article 296(2) TEC)

2.5 Article 133 TEC as Amended by the Treaty of Nice

1. The common commercial policy shall be based on uniform principles, particularly in regard to changes in tariff rates, the conclusion of tariff and trade agreements, the achievement of uniformity in measures of liberalisation, export policy and measures to protect trade such as those to be taken in the event of dumping or subsidies.

2. The Commission shall submit proposals to the Council for implementing the common commercial policy.

3. Where agreements with one or more States or international organisations need to be negotiated, the Commission shall make recommendations to the Council, which shall authorise the Commission to open the necessary negotiations. The Council and the Commission shall be responsible for ensuring that the agreements negotiated are compatible with internal Community policies and rules.

The Commission shall conduct these negotiations in consultation with a special committee appointed by the Council to assist the Commission in this task and within the framework of such directives as the Council may issue to it. The Commission shall report regularly to the special committee on the progress of negotiations.

The relevant provisions of Article 300 shall apply.

4. In exercising the powers conferred upon it by this Article, the Council shall act by a qualified majority.

5. Paragraphs 1 to 4 shall also apply to the negotiation and conclusion of agreements in the fields of trade in services and the commercial aspects of intellectual property, insofar as those agreements are not covered by the said paragraphs and without prejudice to paragraph 6.

By way of derogation from paragraph 4, the Council shall act unanimously when negotiating and concluding an agreement in one of the fields referred to in the first subparagraph, where that agreement includes provisions for which unanimity is required for the adoption of internal rules or where it relates to a field in which the Community has not yet exercised the powers conferred upon it by this Treaty by adopting internal rules.

The Council shall act unanimously with respect to the negotiation and conclusion of a horizontal agreement insofar as it also concerns the preceding subparagraph or the second subparagraph of paragraph 6.

This paragraph shall not affect the right of the Member States to maintain and conclude agreements with third countries or international organisations insofar as such agreements comply with Community law and other relevant international agreements.

6.   An agreement may not be concluded by the Council if it includes provisions which would go beyond the Community's internal powers, in particular by leading to harmonisation of the laws or regulations of the Member States in an area for which this Treaty rules out such harmonisation.

In this regard, by way of derogation from the first subparagraph of paragraph 5, agreements relating to trade in cultural and audiovisual services, educational services, and social and human health services, shall fall within the shared competence of the Community and its Member States. Consequently, in addition to a Community decision taken in accordance with the relevant provisions of Article 300, the negotiation of such agreements shall require the common accord of the Member States. Agreements thus negotiated shall be concluded jointly by the Community and the Member States.

The negotiation and conclusion of international agreements in the field of transport shall continue to be governed by the provisions of Title V and Article 300.

7.   Without prejudice to the first subparagraph of paragraph 6, the Council, acting unanimously on a proposal from the Commission and after consulting the European Parliament, may extend the application of paragraphs 1 to 4 to international negotiations and agreements on intellectual property insofar as they are not covered by paragraph 5.

Appendix 3

The Treaty of Nice Provisions on Enhanced Cooperation

3.1   General Principles

Article 43 TEU

Member States which intend to establish enhanced cooperation between themselves may make use of the institutions, procedures and mechanisms laid down by this Treaty and by the Treaty establishing the European Community provided that the proposed cooperation:

(a)   is aimed at furthering the objectives of the Union and of the Community, at protecting and serving their interests and at reinforcing their process of integration;

(b)   respects the said Treaties and the single institutional framework of the Union;

(c)   respects the *acquis communautaire* and the measures adopted under the other provisions of the said Treaties;

(d)   remains within the limits of the powers of the Union or of the Community and does not concern the areas which fall within the exclusive competence of the Community;

(e)   does not undermine the internal market as defined in Article 14(2) of the Treaty establishing the European Community, or the economic and social cohesion established in accordance with Title XVII of that Treaty;

(f)   does not constitute a barrier to or discrimination in trade between the Member States and does not distort competition between them;

(g)   involves a minimum of eight Member States;

(h)   respects the competences, rights and obligations of those Member States which do not participate therein;

(i)   does not affect the provisions of the Protocol integrating the Schengen acquis into the framework of the European Union;

(j)   is open to all the Member States, in accordance with Article 43b.

Article 43a TEU

Enhanced cooperation may be undertaken only as a last resort, when it has been established within the Council that the objectives of such cooperation cannot be attained within a reasonable period by applying the relevant provisions of the Treaties.

Article 43b TEU

When enhanced cooperation is being established, it shall be open to all Member States. It shall also be open to them at any time, in accordance with Articles 27e and 40b of this Treaty and with Article 11a of the Treaty establishing the European Community, subject to compliance with the basic decision and with the decisions taken within that framework. The Commission and the Member States participating in enhanced cooperation shall ensure that as many Member States as possible are encouraged to take part.

Article 44 TEU

1. For the purposes of the adoption of the acts and decisions necessary for the implementation of enhanced cooperation referred to in Article 43, the relevant institutional provisions of this Treaty and of the Treaty establishing the European Community shall apply. However, while all members of the Council shall be able to take part in the deliberations, only those representing Member States participating in enhanced cooperation shall take part in the adoption of decisions. The qualified majority shall be defined as the same proportion of the weighted votes and the same proportion of the number of the Council members concerned as laid down in Article 205(2) of the Treaty establishing the European Community, and in the second and third subparagraphs of Article 23(2) of this Treaty as regards enhanced cooperation established on the basis of Article 27c. Unanimity shall be constituted by only those Council members concerned.

Such acts and decisions shall not form part of the Union acquis.

2. Member States shall apply, as far as they are concerned, the acts and decisions adopted for the implementation of the enhanced cooperation in which they participate. Such acts and decisions shall be binding only on those Member States which participate in such cooperation and, as appropriate, shall be directly applicable only in those States. Member States which do not participate in such cooperation shall not impede the implementation thereof by the participating Member States.

Article 44a TEU

Expenditure resulting from implementation of enhanced cooperation, other than administrative costs entailed for the institutions, shall be borne by the participating Member States, unless all members of the Council, acting unanimously after consulting the European Parliament, decide otherwise.

Article 45 TEU

The Council and the Commission shall ensure the consistency of activities undertaken on the basis of this Title and the consistency of such activities with the policies of the Union and the Community, and shall cooperate to that end.

3.2 Enhanced Cooperation under the TEC

Article 11 TEC

1.   Member States which intend to establish enhanced cooperation between themselves in one of the areas referred to in this Treaty shall address a request to the Commission, which may submit a proposal to the Council to that effect. In the event of the Commission not submitting a proposal, it shall inform the Member States concerned of the reasons for not doing so.

2.   Authorisation to establish enhanced cooperation as referred to in paragraph 1 shall be granted, in compliance with Articles 43 to 45 of the Treaty on European Union, by the Council, acting by a qualified majority on a proposal from the Commission and after consulting the European Parliament. When enhanced cooperation relates to an area covered by the procedure referred to in Article 251 of this Treaty, the assent of the European Parliament shall be required.

A member of the Council may request that the matter be referred to the European Council. After that matter has been raised before the European Council, the Council may act in accordance with the first subparagraph of this paragraph.

3.   The acts and decisions necessary for the implementation of enhanced cooperation activities shall be subject to all the relevant provisions of this Treaty, save as otherwise provided in this Article and in Articles 43 to 45 of the Treaty on European Union.

Article 11a TEC

Any Member State which wishes to participate in enhanced cooperation established in accordance with Article 11 shall notify its intention to the Council and to the Commission, which shall give an opinion to the Council within three months of the date of receipt of that notification. Within four months of the date of receipt of that notification, the Commission shall take a decision on it, and on such specific arrangements as it may deem necessary.

3.3 Enhanced Cooperation under Title V of the TEU

Article 27a TEU

1. Enhanced cooperation in any of the areas referred to in this Title shall be aimed at safeguarding the values and serving the interests of the Union as a whole by asserting its identity as a coherent force on the international scene. It shall respect:

— the principles, objectives, general guidelines and consistency of the common foreign and security policy and the decisions taken within the framework of that policy;
— the powers of the European Community, and
— consistency between all the Union's policies and its external activities.

2. Articles 11 to 27 and Articles 27b to 28 shall apply to the enhanced cooperation provided for in this Article, save as otherwise provided in Article 27c and Articles 43 to 45.

Article 27b TEU

Enhanced cooperation pursuant to this Title shall relate to implementation of a joint action or a common position. It shall not relate to matters having military or defence implications.

Article 27c TEU

Member States which intend to establish enhanced cooperation between themselves under Article 27b shall address a request to the Council to that effect.

The request shall be forwarded to the Commission and to the European Parliament for information. The Commission shall give its opinion particularly on whether the enhanced cooperation proposed is consistent with Union policies. Authorisation shall be granted by the Council, acting in accordance with the second and third subparagraphs of Article 23(2) and in compliance with Articles 43 to 45.

Article 27d TEU

Without prejudice to the powers of the Presidency or of the Commission, the Secretary-General of the Council, High Representative for the common foreign and security policy, shall in particular ensure that the European Parliament and all members of the Council are kept fully informed of the implementation of enhanced cooperation in the field of the common foreign and security policy.

Article 27e TEU

Any Member State which wishes to participate in enhanced cooperation established in accordance with Article 27c shall notify its intention to the Council and inform the Commission. The Commission shall give an opinion to the Council within three months of the date of receipt of that notification. Within four months of the date of receipt of that notification, the Council shall take a decision on the request and on such specific arrangements as it may deem necessary. The decision shall be deemed to be taken unless the Council, acting by a qualified majority within the same period, decides to hold it in abeyance; in that case, the Council shall state the reasons for its decision and set a deadline for re-examining it.

For the purposes of this Article, the Council shall act by a qualified majority. The qualified majority shall be defined as the same proportion of the weighted votes and the same proportion of the number of the members of the Council concerned as those laid down in the third subparagraph of Article 23(2).

3.4   Enhanced Cooperation under Title VI of the TEU

Article 40 TEU

1.   Enhanced cooperation in any of the areas referred to in this Title shall have the aim of enabling the Union to develop more rapidly into an area of freedom, security and justice, while respecting the powers of the European Community and the objectives laid down in this Title.

2.   Articles 29 to 39 and Articles 40a to 41 shall apply to the enhanced cooperation provided for by this Article, save as otherwise provided in Article 40a and in Articles 43 to 45.

3.   The provisions of the Treaty establishing the European Community concerning the powers of the Court of Justice and the exercise of those powers shall apply to this Article and to Articles 40a and 40b.

Article 40a TEU

1.   Member States which intend to establish enhanced cooperation between themselves under Article 40 shall address a request to the Commission, which may submit a proposal to the Council to that effect. In the event of the Commission not submitting a proposal, it shall inform the Member States concerned of the reasons for not doing so. Those Member States may then submit an initiative to the Council designed to obtain authorisation for the enhanced cooperation concerned.

2.   The authorisation referred to in paragraph 1 shall be granted, in compliance with Articles 43 to 45, by the Council, acting by a qualified majority, on a proposal from the Commission or on the initiative of at least eight Member States, and after consulting the European Parliament. The votes of the members of the Council shall be weighted in accordance with Article 205(2) of the Treaty establishing the European Community.

A member of the Council may request that the matter be referred to the European Council. After that matter has been raised before the European Council, the Council may act in accordance with the first subparagraph of this paragraph.

Article 40b TEU

Any Member State which wishes to participate in enhanced cooperation established in accordance with Article 40a shall notify its intention to the Council and to the Commission, which shall give an opinion to the Council within three months of the date of receipt of that notification, possibly accompanied by a recommendation for such specific arrangements as it may deem necessary for that Member State to become a party to the cooperation in question. The Council shall take a decision on the request within four months of the date of receipt of that notification. The decision shall be deemed to be taken unless the Council, acting by a qualified majority within the same period, decides to hold it in abeyance; in that case, the Council shall state the reasons for its decision and set a deadline for re-examining it.

For the purposes of this Article, the Council shall act under the conditions set out in Article 44(1).

Appendix 4

**Composition, Method of Work and Practical
Arrangements for the Body which Elaborated
the Draft EU Charter of Fundamental Rights**

A. COMPOSITION OF THE BODY

(i) Members

(a) Heads of State or Government of Member States

Fifteen representatives of the Heads of State or Government of Member States.

(b) Commission

One representative of the President of the European Commission.

(c) European Parliament

Sixteen members of the European Parliament to be designated by itself.

(d) National Parliaments

Thirty members of national Parliaments (two from each national Parliament) to be designated by national Parliaments themselves.

Members of the Body may be replaced by alternates in the event of being unable to attend meetings of the Body.

(ii) Chairperson and Vice-Chairpersons of the Body

The Chairperson of the Body shall be elected by the Body. A member of the European Parliament, a member of a national Parliament, and the representative of the President of the European Council if not elected to the Chair, shall act as Vice-Chairpersons of the Body.

The member of the European Parliament acting as Vice-Chairperson shall be elected by the members of the European Parliament serving on the Body. The member of a national Parliament acting as Vice-Chairperson shall be elected by the members of national Parliaments serving on the Body.

(iii) Observers

Two representatives of the Court of Justice of the European Communities to be designated by the Court.

Two representatives of the Council of Europe, including one from the European Court of Human Rights.

(iv) Bodies of the European Union to be invited to give their views

The Economic and Social Committee

The Committee of the Regions

The Ombudsman

(v) **Exchange of views with the applicant States**

An appropriate exchange of views should be held by the Body or by the Chairperson with the applicant States.

(vi) **Other bodies, social groups or experts to be invited to give their views**

Other bodies, social groups and experts may be invited by the Body to give their views.

(vii) **Secretariat**

The General Secretariat of the Council shall provide the Body with secretariat services. To ensure proper coordination, close contacts will be established with the General Secretariat of the European Parliament, with the Commission and, to the extent necessary, with the secretariats of the national Parliaments.

B.   WORKING METHODS OF THE BODY

(i)   **Preparation**

The Chairperson of the Body shall, in close concertation with the Vice-Chairpersons, propose a work plan for the Body and perform other appropriate preparatory work.

(ii)   **Transparency of the proceedings**

In principle, hearings held by the Body and documents submitted at such hearings should be public.

(iii)   **Working groups**

The Body may establish *ad hoc* working groups, which shall be open to all members of the Body.

(iv)   **Drafting**

On the basis of the work plan agreed by the Body, a Drafting Committee composed of the Chairperson, the Vice-Chairpersons and the representative of the Commission and assisted by the General Secretariat of the Council, shall elaborate a preliminary Draft Charter, taking account of drafting proposals submitted by any member of the Body.

Each of the three Vice-Chairpersons shall regularly consult with the respective component part of the Body from which he or she emanates.

(v)   **Elaboration of the Draft Charter by the Body**

When the Chairperson, in close concertation with the Vice-Chairpersons, deems that the text of the draft Charter elaborated by the Body can eventually be subscribed to by all the parties, it shall be forwarded to the European Council through the normal preparatory procedure.

C. PRACTICAL ARRANGEMENTS

The Body shall hold its meetings in Brussels, alternately in the Council and the European Parliament buildings.

A complete language regime shall be applicable for sessions of the Body.

Bibliography

All official IGC documents are publicly available on the website of the Council of the European Union (www.ue.eu.int). Only those documents cited in this book are listed below under 'IGC'. The tables featured in Chapters 4 and 6 were produced by the author during the Conference.

Agence Europe
    2000   'Journée politique – Sommet de Biarritz', 25 October 2000, p. 3.

Baldwin, R., E. Berglöf, F. Giavazzi and M. Widgrén
    2000   'EU Reforms for Tomorrow's Europe' *Discussion Paper No. 2623*, Centre for Economic Policy Research, London, November.

Barnier, M.
    2000   'La grande illusion du droit de veto', *Le Figaro*, 27 November.

Best, E.
    2000   'The Debate over the Weighting of Votes: The Mis-presentation of Representation?', in Best *et al.* 2000: 105-30.

Best, E., M. Gray and A. Stubb (eds.)
    2000   *Rethinking the European Union: IGC 2000 and Beyond* (Maastricht: EIPA).

Börzel, T.A., and T. Risse
    2000   'Who is Afraid of a European Federation? How to Constitutionalise a Multi-level Governance System', in C. Joerges, Y. Mény and J.H.H. Weiler (eds.), *What Kind of Constitution for What Kind of Polity?: Responses to Joschka Fischer* (Cambridge, MA: Harvard Law School): 45-58.

Burgess, M.
    2000   *Federalism and European Union: The Building of Europe, 1950–2000* (London: Routledge).

Corbett, R., F. Jacobs and M. Shackleton
    2000   *The European Parliament* (4th edn; London, John Harper).

Council of the European Union
    1999a   'Operation of the Council with an Enlarged Union in Prospect', *Report by the Working Party set up by the Secretary-General of the Council*, doc. SN 2139/99, March.
    1999b   Presidency Conclusions, Berlin European Council, 24–25 March.
    1999c   Presidency Conclusions, Cologne European Council, 3–4 June.

1999d   'Efficient Institutions after Enlargement: Options for the Intergovernmental Conference' *Presidency Report to the Helsinki European Council*,
doc. 13636/99, December.

1999e   Presidency Conclusions, Helsinki European Council, 10–11 December.

2000a   Presidency Conclusions, Feira European Council, 19–20 June.

2000b   'Consolidated Version of the Treaties', Vols. 1 and 2, *doc. SN 1845/00*,
July 2000.

Court of Auditors

2000a   'Contribution to the IGC', *IGC document CONFER 4738/00*, April.

2000b   'Supplementary Contribution to the IGC', *IGC document CONFER
4794/00*, October.

Dashwood, A.

1996   'The Limits of European Community Powers', *European Law Review* 1.2
April: 113-28.

Dehaene, J.-L., D. Simon and R. von Weizsäcker

1999   'The Institutional Implications of Enlargement', *Report to the European
Commission*, 18 October.

De L'Ecotais, M.

1996a   'La pondération des voix au Conseil des Ministres de la Communauté
européenne', *Revue du Marché Commun et de l'Union européenne*, No.
398, May: 388-93.

1996b   'De l'Europe des six à l'Europe des douze: une évolution réussie', *Revue
du Marché Commun et de l'Union européenne*, No. 401, September: 617-
20.

1997   'L'Europe de douze à quinze: l'échec', *Revue du Marché Commun et de
l'Union européenne*, No. 408, May: 324-27.

De Schoutheete, P.

2000   *The Case for Europe: Unity, Diversity, and Democracy in the European
Union* (London: Lynne Rienner).

Dinan, D.

1999   *Ever Closer Union: An Introduction to European Integration* (Basingstoke: Macmillan).

Due, O.

2000   'Report by the Study Group on the Future of the EC Judicial System',
European Commission, January.

Edwards, G., and D. Spence

1997   *The European Commission* (London: Cartermill).

European Commission

1999   'Commission's Contribution to Preparations for the IGC', *COM(99) 592
final*, 2 December.

2000a   'Adapting the Institutions to Make a Success of Enlargement: Opinion of
the European Commission to the Intergovernmental Conference', *IGC
document CONFER 4701/00*, January.

2000b   'Additional Contribution to the IGC on Reforming the Community
Judicial Architecture', *IGC document CONFER 4724/00,* March.

2000c   *Eurobarometer 52*, April.

2000d   'Commission Communication: A Basic Treaty for the EU', *IGC
document CONFER 4763/00*.

European Community (EC)
    1999   'Joint Declaration of the European Parliament, the Council and the Commission on Practical Arrangements for the New Codecision Procedure', *Official Journal of the EC, C 148*, 28 May.

European Court of Justice (ECJ)
    1986   Case 294/83, *Parti Ecologiste, 'Les Verts' v. European Parliament* [1986] ECR 1,339-1, 365.
    2000   'Contribution by the Court of Justice and the Court of First Instance to the Intergovernmental Conference', *IGC document CONFER/VAR/3964/00*.

European Parliament
    2000   'Resolution on the European Parliament's Proposals for the *IGC' IGC document CONFER 4736/00*, April.

European University Institute (EUI)
    2000   *Reorganisation of the Treaties: Final Report and Draft Basic Treaty*, (Florence: Robert Schuman Centre for Advanced Studies).

Galloway, D.
    1999   'Agenda 2000: Packaging the Deal', *Journal of Common Market Studies* 37, Annual Review Keynote Article: 9-35.

Golub, J.
    1999   'In the Shadow of the Vote?: Decision Making in the European Community', *International Organisation* 53.4: 733-64.
    2000   'Institutional Reform and Decision-making in the European Union', *Paper for the Political Studies Association-UK 50th Annual Conference*, London, 10–13 April.

Hayes-Renshaw, F., and H. Wallace
    1997   *The Council of Ministers* (London: Macmillan).

Hosli, M.
    1996   'Coalitions and Power: Effects of Qualified Majority Voting in the Council of the European Union', *Journal of Common Market Studies* 34.2: 255-73.

IGC
    2000a   'The Commission', Presidency Note to IGC Representatives, *IGC document CONFER 4744/00*.
    2000b   'Weighting of Votes in the Council', Presidency Note to IGC Representatives, *IGC document CONFER 4745/00*.
    2000c   'Intergovernmental Conference on Institutional Reform', Presidency Report to the Feira European Council, *IGC document CONFER 4750/00*.
    2000d   'Enhanced Cooperation in the Second *Pillar'* Proposal to the IGC by the Spanish delegation, *IGC document CONFER 4760/00*.
    2000e   'The Competence to Accede to the European Convention for the Protection of Human Rights and Fundamental Freedoms, signed in Rome on 4 November 1950', Proposal to the IGC by the Finnish delegation, *IGC document CONFER 4775/00*.
    2000f   'Quality Majority Voting', Contribution to the IGC from Ireland, *IGC document CONFER 4778/00*.
    2000g   'Position Paper on Closer Cooperation', Paper submitted by the German and Italian delegations, *IGC document CONFER 4783/1/00 REV 1*.

2000h　　　'European Security and Defence Policy', Proposals by Italy, Belgium, the Netherlands and Luxembourg, *IGC document CONFER 4788/00*.

2000i　　　'Incorporation of a Reference to Eurojust in the Treaty', Proposal to the IGC by the French delegation, *IGC document CONFER 4806/1/00 REV 1*.

Jacobs, F.

2000　　　'IGC 2000: Challenges for the European Parliament', in Best *et al.* 2000: 53-60.

Lord, C.

1998　　　*Democracy in the European Union* (Sheffield: Sheffield Academic Press).

Ludlow, P.

2001　　　'The European Council at Nice: Neither Triumph nor Disaster', *Background Paper*, CEPS International Advisory Council, 1–2 February.

McDonagh, B.

1998　　　*Original Sin in a Brave New World: An Account of the Negotiation of the Treaty of Amsterdam* (Dublin: Institute for European Affairs)

Moïsi, D.

2001　　　'Caught between Enlargement and Globalisation', *Financial Times*, 15 January.

Nugent, N.

1999　　　*The Government and Politics of the European Union* (London: Macmillan).

2001　　　*The European Commission* (Basingstoke: Palgrave).

Patten, C.

2000　　　'Souveraineté et démocratie: Réflexions d'un britannique européen', *Commentaires No. 92*: 751-62.

Pernice, I.

2000　　　'Kompetenzabrenzung im Europäischen Verfassungsverbund' *Juristen Zeitung N° 18 55*, 15 September: 866-76.

Pescatore, P.

1986　　　'L'acte unique européen – Observations critiques', *Europe Documents*, Bulletin No. 1397, 27 March (Brussels: Agence Europe).

Peterson, J., and E. Bomberg

1999　　　*Decision-Making in the European Union* (London: Macmillan).

Petite, M.

2000　　　'The IGC and the European Commission' in Best *et al.* 2000: 61-66.

Philippart, E., and M. Sie Dhian Ho

2000　　　'The Pros and Cons of Closer Co-operation: Argumentation and Recommendations', *Paper for the Netherlands Scientific Council for government policy*, The Hague, February.

Piris, J-C.

1999　　　'Does the European Union Have a Constitution? Does it Need One?', *European Law Review* 24: 557-85.

Quermonne, J.-L.

1999　　　'L'Union européenne en quête d'institutions légitimes et efficaces', *Rapport du Groupe présidé par Jean-Louis Quermonne* (Paris: documentation française): 104.

Riccardi, F.

2001   'Ce qui a été décidé à Nice à propos de la Commission européenne ne résout pas les problèmes et recèle un danger grave', *Bulletin quotidien* No. 7883, 18 January (Brussels: Agence Europe).

Shackleton, M.

2000   'The Politics of Codecision', *Journal of Common Market Studies,* 38.2 June: 325-42.

Shaw, J.

2000   *Law of the European Union* (London: Palgrave).

Stubb, A.

1998   *Flexible Integration and the Amsterdam Treaty: Negotiating Differentiation in the 1996–1997 IGC*, PhD thesis (London: LSE).

2000   'Dealing with Flexibility in the IGC' in Best *et al.* (2000): 145-58.

2001   *From Amsterdam to Nice and Beyond: Negotiating Flexible Integration in the European Union* (London: Macmillan, forthcoming).

Teasdale, A.

1999   'The Luxembourg compromise' in Westlake 1999: 104-10.

Wallace, H.

2000   'Some Observations on the Illusions of Institutional Balance and the Representation of States', in Best *et al.* 2000: 209-18.

Weatherill, S.

1999   'If I'd Wanted You to Understand I Would Have Explained it Better: What Is the Purpose of the Provisions on Close Co-operation Introduced by the Treaty of Amsterdam?', in D. O'Keeffe and P. Twomey (eds.), *Legal Issues of the Amsterdam Treaty* (Oxford: Hart): 21-40.

Weiler, J.H.H.

1999   *The Constitution of Europe* (Cambridge: Cambridge University Press).

2000   'IGC 2000: The Constitutional Agenda' in Best *et al.* 2000: 219-36.

2001   'Epilogue—Fischer: The Dark Side', in C. Joerges, Y. Mény and J.H.H. Weiler (eds.), *What Kind of Constitution for What Kind of Polity?: Responses to Joschka Fischer* (Cambridge, MA: Harvard Law School): 235-47.

Westlake, M.

1999   *The Council of the European Union* (London: Cartermill).

Winkler, M.

1998   'Coalition Sensitive Voting Power in the Council of Ministers: The Case of Eastern Enlargement', *Journal of Common Market Studies,* 36.3: 391-404.

General Index

Index of Authors